Wired to Listen

WIRED TO LISTEN

What Kids Learn from What We Say

Muffie Wiebe Waterman, PhD

To my mom, Mary Wiebe

whose words and voice guide me, even now

Contents

Preface

My whole life, I have been surrounded by language. My father is a university professor who can strike up a conversation with anyone, of any station, in any part of the world. My mother had a lovely speaking and singing voice, the most beautiful smile, and a ready and friendly comment for anyone nearby.

I grew up being respected, spoken to, and even consulted about my opinions. This obviously had a formative influence on my perspective for this book, however the book doesn't spring from my experience alone. It draws heavily from the world of research and from masterful classroom practice.

While writing, I remembered a story my mom told me in my twenties: She and I took part in a study when I was a baby. We lived in a university town and my mom signed us up. When we arrived at the lab, she was amused that all they wanted her to do was play with me as she normally would. She said she happily babbled away to me and enjoyed a nice, rather uneventful, time.

Afterward, the researchers explained what they were studying. It turned out they were looking to see how mothers spoke to their babies. They had expected to find that most or all did—just as my mother had. They had been shocked to find that many of the mothers spoke hardly a word to their baby. My mom was surprised to find that something she did so naturally was both rare and, quite possibly, essential.

Perhaps I was predisposed by my mom to think that talking to kids matters. Maybe this book, in some way, is a gift to her.

I just know in my heart that what we say to kids matters deeply. And I am so excited to show you how.

Introduction

Water what you want to grow

Walking into my daughter's fourth-grade classroom for the first time, I was struck by a prominently placed handwritten sign:

Be careful of your thoughts, they become your words.
Be careful of your words, they become your actions.
Be careful of your actions, they become your habits.
Be careful of your habits, they become your character.
—*Author unknown*

It seemed like ancient wisdom, but I had never heard it. The sign was artfully lettered and hung in a central place in the classroom. I felt it offered a great message for these nine- and ten-year-old children, poised as they were in fourth grade to become more independent: you are in charge of where you are headed.

Children at this age are emerging from the primary years of schooling. They are aware of being different from their just-past eight-year-old selves. They are bigger and more self-possessed, though still very young. They are beginning to understand sarcasm. They are thirsty for control. And yet, as any elementary-school teacher will tell you, they are still oh-so-malleable.

What I love about the message on this sign is that it is so simple: Life starts in our heads. Our worlds are created out of our thoughts. Therefore, the things that influence our thoughts are important.

This is where what we say to children kicks in.

I'm starting the book here because I think this quote gets at the heart of why our words to children matter. What we say to children—when they're babies, toddlers, and teenagers—becomes their inner voice. It becomes and shapes their thoughts.

About a month before finishing this book, this stunningly apropos conversation between a friend and two other parents showed up in my Facebook feed:

> My daughter told me that she heard my voice in her head while having a difficult discussion with a friend. That really made me realize how important this parenting stuff is. What we say becomes part of our kids' inner dialogues.
>
>> Yes....Sadly my mother's voice "in my head" is not at all helpful to me. It is to be overcome and not embraced. I have always been inspired by your relationship with your children. It has helped me imagine how if I had been raised by such a conscious present loving mom I would shine so brightly as your kids.
>>
>> That's absolutely true. Even when you don't think they are listening what you're saying sticks...a very good reason to be careful what we say.

This book explores how what we say—and the way we say it—matters to children. With the same intentions as Adele Faber and Elaine Mazlish's classic book for parents, *How to Talk So Kids Will Listen & Listen So Kids Will Talk*, or Peter Johnston's book for teachers, *Choice Words*, I show how what we say shapes children's understanding of the world, and also themselves. Here, I draw together a unique combination of current and classic research, classroom practice, and family stories, to offer parents, teachers, grandparents and others a view into how kids are learning from us when we speak to them. What we say shapes the way kids will perceive the world, and how they choose to act in it.

Practice Makes "Better"

The perfect is the enemy of the good.

—*Attributed to Voltaire*

"Practice makes perfect" pervades our culture. It is parroted by teachers and parents everywhere. It's meant to be encouraging or motivating, but for many people it's stultifying. Perfection is so out of reach that "practice makes perfect" is not actually helpful. I find it grating. Voltaire's quote from the 1700s suggests people have been arguing the counterpoint for at least a few hundred years. Yet the chant of "practice makes perfect" persists.

Is *perfect* the real goal? How many of us will ever become that? More than that, for me, the phrase simultaneously ridicules true excellence (which is not attainable by all) and true effort (which will not lead all of us to perfection).

"Practice makes better" is a phrase that took my breath away when I first heard it at Mulberry School—the idea that we should keep at it, keep trying, because we *will* see improvement. In fact, that's the only way we will. My children's third-grade teacher lives by this mantra. She coaches all her students with it, and they have the best attitudes I have ever seen in a classroom. Everything is about doing. Everything is about being in the now, working on things, seeing them change, and enjoying the doing. Her students are productive—and excited about learning.

This idea—focus on improving, not perfection—is a game changer. It frees up creative potential, and joy, and it removes the stress of performance. It's very much in line with Carol Dweck's growth mindset work. In her widely read book, *Mindset: The New Psychology of Success*, Dweck spells out the difference between a fixed mindset, which holds that intelligence and success are innate and due to inborn talent, and a growth mindset, which holds that intelligence and success come from sustained effort.

Her years of research show that children (and adults) who operate from a growth mindset are happier, adjust better to stress, and succeed more in their lives.

"Practice makes better" gets at the central idea of this book: what we say shapes how we see things. The beautiful and simple truth is that one small word change can shift the meaning, and impact, of what we say. This is especially true of what we say to children, since they are forming their understanding of the world. The words we use and the way we say them bring into being children's worldview and their concept of themselves.

The idea that we can look differently at how we talk to kids can sound like welcome news, or it can unleash a lot of frustration and disappointment. In my experience, there are two big reasons the parents of younger children seek out advice more frequently than do parents of older kids: (1) As newer, less experienced parents, they're more comfortable (or at least less uncomfortable!) feeling they don't know what they're doing, and (2) they don't have the burden of feeling as if they've made mistakes. It feels awful to think we've screwed up—especially with our children, for whom we have every best wish.

Rather than feeling burdened by this, I hope you will feel liberated—that the stories and ideas here will help you feel encouraged and able to try something new. There's no point in being upset about what you might have done better in the past. It's never too late to start doing things better! I hope that in seeing what I have laid out—from research, master practitioners, my teaching, my own parenting, and stories from many others—you will find a new and exciting possibility ahead of you: What you say matters.

Water What You Want to Grow

I used to start my cognitive development classes off with this phrase: "Water what you want to grow." I love it because it really is that simple. Water it, and it will flourish. Don't water it, and it will shrivel and die. "You reap what you sow" is the same idea. You get what you plant, or water.

I like these growth metaphors regarding children. That's what we're doing after all: growing adults. So *water what you want to grow*. Because here's the thing: the flip side is also true. *Whatever* you water is what will grow. It doesn't matter if you like it or dislike it, want it or don't, or even realize that you're watering. If you give something attention, if you do it and repeat, it will be taken up by kids.

This is true whether you know you're doing it or not. Because what babies and children pay attention to from birth is our voices and our words. Obviously, they also pay attention to our nonverbal communication, but our words are particularly powerful. And our hidden beliefs and thoughts slip out through our language.

Take this, for example: When a child gets hurt, what do parents say afterward? In the aftermath of a serious injury, parents in one study were **four times more likely to tell their daughters to be careful than their sons.** Which is interesting, given that medical researchers point out that boys are *much more likely* to be injured.

Canadian psychologists Elizabeth O'Neal, Jodie Plumert, and Carole Petersen interviewed eighty-seven families whose child (ages three to sixteen) had been in the ER, to find out what kinds of conversations they'd had in the week or two following the accident.

As you might expect, the majority of the parents (70 percent of the full sample, or sixty-one parents) had talked to their child about how to prevent that kind of injury in the future. And among them were a variety of approaches, with about half reporting two or more approaches. The most frequent thing discussed (by 54 percent of these sixty-one parents who discussed prevention) was to give the child new ideas and strategies for accomplishing the same thing. Parents were tied between just urging their child to be more careful and simply not to do it again (38 percent for both). I was personally delighted to see that *explaining why* it was dangerous to begin with was part of what some parents were saying (33 percent) and that giving such explanations became more likely as the child's age increased.

Yet in this mix, parents urged their *girls* to be more careful— four times more often than their boys—despite the boys' taking bigger risks and incurring more injuries. In general, research has shown that parents *look for* and *accept* higher risk from boys. This creates a feedback loop that is highly gendered. Boys take risks and are rewarded—or at least not admonished. Girls take risks and are admonished—or at least told to be more careful. This verbal guidance influences the actions kids take in the future.

Over time, these words establish patterns and mindsets about risk and injury: mindsets that are different for boys and for girls, based on what they've been told by parents who have no idea that they are talking to their daughters and sons differently. So, for example, if we want girls to be bold, we have to stop telling them—disproportionately—to be careful.

Water what you want to grow.

Brain Science

Brain-imaging technology has given us a brand-new look at how the human brain works. We can now get a glimpse into the neural mechanisms of the brain. And **it is quite clear that where our attention goes, the biology follows.**

Anytime we pay attention, a chain of neurons fires. When we repeatedly pay attention to the same thing, that same chain fires, over and over again. This repeated signaling across the same communicating neurons establishes a kind of pathway. Think of a plaza where the sidewalks have been supplanted by shortcuts worn down in the grass. These shortcuts show the paths most frequently walked. In fact, human-centered, design-oriented landscape planners will hold out before laying the hardscape. They'll wait and see where the traffic patterns actually show up and then build the sidewalks where they're needed.

It's the same idea with our brains. Any pathway that repeatedly gets used becomes more defined. Neuroscientists have taken to labeling this feature of our brain development as "neurons that fire together, wire together." What this literally means is that repeated firing lays down additional neural circuitry. The neurons become more easily accessible to one another. One way this happens is through the laying down of additional protective coating. This coating is a fatty tissue called *myelin*. Myelin acts as an insulator, which means that the signal being passed along gets there more efficiently and more swiftly.

A quick four-step intro to basic brain anatomy may help here. You've probably heard the term *neurochemistry* and also the term *EEG*—electroencephalogram—which reads the electrical impulses across the scalp. Yet you may not have appreciated until now that our brains are both chemical *and* electrical organs. So consider the following about the brain:

1. Most of the cells in our brain are neuron cells. Their job is to pass information along to other cells in the body (either other neurons or cells that make up our muscles, digestion, etc.).

2. Each neuron has a long tail coming off one end—the *axon.* An electrical impulse passes along it. But the whacky part is that neurons don't pass their electrical signals to each other directly. In fact, neurons don't even touch each other!

3. At the end of each axon, there's a chemical release, in which the information the neuron is passing gets changed entirely. What was electricity becomes chemistry. Neurochemicals then drip from the end of the axon's buttons onto a neighboring neuron.

4. The next neuron absorbs these neurochemicals through its *dendrites.* The chemical information is then converted back to an electrical signal. This signal is shot down the axon, where it will again be transformed into chemicals.

This astounding process of electricity $\rightarrow$ chemistry $\rightarrow$ electricity $\rightarrow$ chemistry happens between every neuron in the pathway. In the time it takes you to read this sentence, that process occurs millions of times. It's staggering to consider.

What makes us capable of *thinking* is the fact that some neural pathways get better defined over time. The more we practice—and remember, practice makes better, not perfect—the more the set of neurons in that particular pathway become adapted to each other. That's what "neurons that fire together, wire together" means. **Attention habits actually change the biological structure of the brain.**

One of the biggest names in neuroscience today is Rick Hanson, a Senior Fellow at UC Berkeley's Greater Good Science Center. Hanson's area of research interest is meditation and mindfulness. He has written several books, including *Buddha's Brain: The Practical Neuroscience of Happiness, Love, and Wisdom*. From his work in neuropsychology, Hanson argues flat out that "you are what you pay attention to." And what is it we know babies and children are paying attention to? Human voices speaking human language sounds. (More on this in Chapter 1, "Small Shift, Big Impact."

This is the heart of why this book matters. Babies are listening to everything we say. They are taking our words in, and it is literally shaping the structure of their brain.

When we understand this, it gives us a different perspective on what we're doing when we spend time with children. It gives us an important tool in helping kids—our own children, our students, or just kids in our lives—grow up well. We want the best for them. Let's make sure we are giving it to them.

How to Use this Book

This book is the story of how what we say shapes how kids think. This story is built using examples from parents and classrooms, current research on child development and brain science, and suggestions to try at the end of each section.

This book is *not* going to tell you what you're doing wrong. We are all doing things wrong. You don't need me or anyone else pointing those out. Instead, this book is going to ask you what you want for the children in your life—and it's going to show you how to talk so that those things come into being and bear fruit.

The way we talk to children tells them what is important. It shapes what they think. It shapes who they become. To that end, I have one note about the way *I* talk in this book, specifically regarding pronouns. As I show in the next section, gendered pronouns carry more bias than we tend to realize. Because this book is about how our language shapes understanding, it is important to me to avoid amplifying gender bias. Throughout the book, when I refer to a real child, I use the appropriate pronoun *he* or *she*. When discussing children in general, though, I use the gender-neutral pronouns *they, their, them*. This use of *they* as an indeterminate singular has centuries of use behind it. It's also in keeping with the thrust of the research in this book.

You can get the most out of this book by reading it two ways:

1. With optimism

This book is about shining a light on things you might not have considered. It's not about telling you everything you're doing wrong. As I mentioned earlier, I share research and stories—from my teaching, from K-12 classrooms, and my own parenting—to help make sense of it. And there are suggestions of things to try at the end of many sections.

2. With curiosity

Be open to seeing patterns in the way you speak to children. Be open to trying the ideas at the end of each section. I've made them short and doable. If you explore them, you will see more deeply into how you talk to kids. It doesn't mean you have to question everything you ever say. The book will point to areas you can think about.

The good news is that human brains are malleable and influence can shift us to healthier patterns at any time. Why not start today?

Kids are fun. Being with kids can and should be a lot of fun. I believe the ideas in this book will help you have a better time with the kids in your life while also helping you ensure that they can grow into strong, wonderful adults.

1

Small Shift, Big Impact

Three examples

I want to start by showing you examples of how what we say has a hidden impact. It's likely no one has ever told you this, and maybe you've never thought about it: even the simplest words can have astonishing effects.

Example 1: *But* Versus *And*

B-U-T. Three small letters. Yet they pack a wallop. We hear it from kids all the time. "But I want it!" "But you said I could!"

You probably haven't noticed all the places *but* shows up in your own words. And here's why it's worth noticing: **but discounts everything that comes before it.** It denies or disputes the worth or value of what came before, asserting that what comes after is actually the truth—or is more important.

And, on the other hand, is inclusive. It allows for the truth of what came before, while also expanding to include the truth of what comes after.

Imagine a parent is heading out to work and sees their young child's face crumple. Maybe you're that parent. It can be hard to leave under those circumstances. Add to the mix that you're already late or have an important meeting with your boss, and it's harder still to be present for your child. At times like this, parents often yell, plead, threaten, or bribe. What could we set up instead? It would be great to have something better to say!

So just for a moment, as you read this, pause—and actually say these two sentences out loud:

"I love you, *but* I need to leave now to go to work."

"I love you, *and* I need to leave now to go to work."

Children hear "but" as an erasure of their needs. It's also a reminder that grown-ups have all the control (which we do; there's no need to rub their noses in it). If their needs are erased, they don't feel heard or understood, and as a result, they don't feel safe. It may seem like a small, subtle difference. It is. And these small differences add up over a childhood of talking.

"Yes, you want that, **but** you can't have it."

If you are the child on the receiving end of this, what is there to do but be upset, argue, throw a tantrum, or be mad that you've been controlled and denied something you want? Young children and teens find it easier to be mad at their parent than to deal with their disappointment. Using *but* just hands them that opportunity on a silver platter.

"Yes, you want that, **and** you can't have it."

Yikes. If you're the child, you want it *and* your parent sees that plus they sympathize. And yet it's not going to happen, so what to do? Possibly melt down, but there's less to resist here. You could still be mad at your parent, but it's not as easy. It's actually easier just to be sad. That way you can still be comforted (younger children) or escape with some dignity (teens).

And is affiliative. It creates an *us* rather than a *you versus me*. Because it is affiliative, *and* avoids the power struggles that so many families contend with. Imagine a child who doesn't whine or throw tantrums. It is actually possible!

You can even play with this difference mathematically and symbolically as well, considering the difference between the mathematical symbols ∩ and ∪.

But = ∩ *intersection of sets*
And = ∪ *union of sets*

You can see these symbols as horseshoes, so the negating, eroding *but* leaks out its good luck, while the inclusive, affiliative *and* holds its good luck in. They even look like emoticons. And it doesn't take a PhD to tell you which one is more appealing.

But versus *and*. Shifting that one simple word changes so much on the receiving end for children:

- What they hear
- How they react
- What they're able to self-regulate
- How quickly they recover

It's almost like magic. If you start when they're babies, this will work like a charm from the very beginning. If you have children or teens—things won't transform overnight when you begin to use *and*. They will change though. And you'll see it.

Things to Try

1. For today, just listen for places where people use the word *but*. Notice how often it is used.

2. When you hear *but* enter the conversation, test out if you think it limits what comes afterward.

3. Try out a couple of versions for yourself. How do they feel?

Example 2: "Yes, and" versus "Yes, but"

Here's an example of *but* versus *and* at work. And it's really at "work," since this comes from the corporate world.

The Stanford d.school (short for Design School) is one of the world's preeminent sources and leaders in advancing design thinking, led by IDEO founder David Kelley. In addition to the courses and degree programs offered, d.school staff lead workshops for companies, organizations, and schools looking to change how they do their work.

Design thinking has been getting more attention over the past ten to fifteen years. David Kelley is one of its earliest proponents, often credited with starting the movement. As the founder of the design school, he helped create a program that reflects and inspires the mainstays of design process. One of the hallmarks of good design thinking is that it allows for openness of ideas. For ideas to flow, people have to feel free to speak their mind, free from judgment and free from constraints. This is where *but* versus *and* comes in.

The d.school incorporates an exercise in its workshops to get at the power of *and*. In the first part of the exercise, groups are asked to work on a problem together—it could be as simple as planning a party. Each person in the group is required to contribute ideas, and the group is given a brief period of time to work, say, three minutes. The catch is that after anyone has added their thought, the next person must begin their contribution with "yes, but . . . " The facilitator opens the exercise, and everyone is supposed to start jumping in with their contributions. It runs something like this:

"Let's make it a theme party!"
"Yes, but I don't like themes. They get so kitcshy."

"Yes, but a lot of people like them."

"Yes, but we could make it Hawaiian and everyone could wear silly shirts!"

"Yes, but not everyone has a Hawaiian shirt."

"Yes, but we could have a tub out and people could grab one if they need it."

"Yes, but would we have to serve Hawaiian food? Nobody likes poi."

It is amazing how stifling the use of *but* is. It's hard to be creative with your ideas. It's hard to articulate your ideas. It's hard even to *have* ideas. And the energy in the group plummets almost immediately. No fun. No good work done. No group cohesion and very little progress made.

In the second part of the exercise, groups are then told that they should work on the same problem together, and this time, after anyone has added their thought, the next person must begin their contribution with "Yes, and . . . " The facilitator opens the exercise with the same prompt, and again everyone is supposed to start jumping in with their contributions. The exercise is instantly illuminating:

"Let's make it a theme party!"

"Yes, and—ooh—let's make it a Hawaiian theme!"

"Yes, and we could have everyone wear Hawaiian shirts!"

"Yes, and if they don't have them, we could have a tub of them. And those plastic leis!"

"Yes, and we could have great decorations, with torches and flowers."

"Yes, and we could have Hawaiian food—and maybe other things, in case people don't like it."

"Yes, and we could make it a potluck!"

"Yes, and . . . " opens up ideas. People start adding in their thoughts more quickly, new and different ideas appear, the group starts laughing, and the energy palpably increases. Way more fun, lots of ideas (good and kooky). The group starts to coalesce around shared problem solving, and is energized as they move into the next phase of the workshop. It's a great exercise because its lessons are quickly and easily learned. *But* is a conversation/idea/vitality stopper. *And* will take you places.

Things to Try

1. Today, notice how you add on to what others say. Notice if you use *but* and reflect on what it adds and how you feel—both about what the other person is doing and about what you are adding to the conversation.

2. When you hear yourself use *but* with a child, try saying the thing again using *and*. See if it feels any different.

3. The next time you catch yourself using *but* with a child you work with or care for, ask them how they feel about what you just said. And just listen to them.

Example 3: "Boys and Girls"

Young children love picture books, and they love being read to. Even in today's digital life, I strongly encourage reading to kids. It gives them time with an adult, and exposure to ideas and vocabulary they wouldn't come to on their own. And of all books to read, I strongly recommend young children's picture books. Picture books have some of the most gorgeous artwork anywhere, and you can have it in your home or classroom for pennies compared to the cost of other art. Picture books also let you bring in the world in ways you might not be able to otherwise, showing kids people and places they might never see.

Yet despite these terrific benefits, picture books also carry a message about the world that is easily missed: Picture books are more heavily about boy characters. White boy characters, at that.

Even in picture books with animal characters, you'll find the characters are predominantly male. Often, entirely male. Why is that? Can't disruptive dinosaurs and playful pandas be girls?

This isn't about being politically correct. I'm not marking each page in every picture book and saying it has to be fifty-fifty. Just as I'm not counting heads and saying there has to be a quota of brown ducks, yellow ducklings, white geese, and black swans. Picture books have strong visuals but words are underneath it all.

This is about understanding that our words teach kids what to think.

Kids in preschool are already aware that they are girls or boys. Gender is one of the earliest pieces of self-understanding they develop. It's right up there with knowing their age and their name, and it's in place by preschool. *"I three! I a girl!"*

Quick side note: In child development, the idea that each person develops their gender identity was initially proposed back in the 1960s by Lawrence Kohlberg. Through his research, he categorized a set of three well-documented stages that children go through, from initially identifying their gender by about age three (*gender identity*), to understanding that it will stay the same over time (*gender stability*), and then to understanding it won't change just because you change outward appearance (*gender constancy*). My students often asked about the impact of social changes on this process of understanding. I do wonder what the technological advance of gender reassignment surgery, and the social opening up of gender as nonbinary, will mean.

My curiosity about the impact of gendered *language* started when our daughter was a baby. I was already familiar with a fair amount of research on gender socialization as part of child development (and I'll say more on that in Chapter 10, regarding research on *cognitive demand*). I started noticing how people talked about clothing for girls versus boys. Shopping for toys and for clothing, I was put off by how gendered all the choices were. (I shopped for my baby daughter in the boys' sections because they had red and blue there.) You may have seen the viral videos of young kids in the "pink" aisles at toy stores. It's overwhelming.

Still, I was surprised a couple of years later when one of my daughter's preschool teachers stressed that **they didn't use the phrase "boys and girls" in the classroom because it had been shown to increase gender-stereotyped behavior.** I didn't chase down the article, but the idea lingered with me, and I even shared it with other educators.

Gender and He/She—What Does the Research Show?

A 2010 study caught my eye, because it renewed this claim that using the phrase "boys and girls" in a classroom leads kids to have more gender-stereotyped behavior. It was published in the field's preeminent research journal, *Child Development*, and what impressed me was that it measured a fairly big impact over a fairly short period.

Researchers Lacey Hilliard and Lynn Liben at Penn State University conducted a two-week study with fifty-seven preschoolers. Children were assigned to either a classroom that *avoided* the use of gender terms or a classroom that *made deliberate use* of them. Neither classroom included direct comparisons between the sexes, so it wasn't that the kids were hearing boys and girls compared. Nor did any of the teachers voice stereotypes of differences between the sexes. It was simply that in one class the teachers used the phrase "boys and girls" to address the children, as so many teachers do.

(Liben is a colleague of Rebecca Bigler, whose 1995 study on preschool and gender language may have been the one my daughter's teacher knew about. That study, also published in *Child Development*, found that children in classrooms that emphasize gender show more gender-stereotyped behavior.)

Since it was known that being in a classroom with gendered language has an impact, the 2010 study sought to see how quickly that might happen. Before and after their experiment, Hilliard and Liben surveyed the children's beliefs and observed who they played with. Despite the fact the study was *only two weeks* long, children for whom gender was made salient "showed significantly increased gender stereotypes, less positive ratings of other-sex peers, and decreased play with other-sex peers."

In other words, children who heard the gendered terms over those two weeks were *more likely to engage in gender-stereotyped behavior*. After only two weeks. Yikes!

There's a theory for this: developmental intergroup theory. In previous work, Liben and Bigler (2006) laid out the four factors involved in forming stereotypes or prejudice: "(1) perceptual discriminability of social groups, (2) proportional group size, (3) explicit labeling and use of social groups, and (4) implicit use of social groups."

They go on to say that *while perceptual characteristics are the most likely to be used in stereotyping, on their own, they aren't enough.* This makes sense, right? "Perceptual characteristics" are the things we can see. It's much easier to stereotype based on a difference we can actually see than one that is less visible. But the research shows that it takes one of the other three factors to kick it from being something you just *notice* to something you *act on.* In other words, only when we add one of the other factors to an obvious difference—either labeling a minority status, labeling groups differently, or outright segregating groups—will kids go from noticing the difference to acting on it.

What do children do about these differences? Does it change how they act or what they believe about other people?

I've long taught my students that kids will notice perceptual differences. How could they not? Young children are fascinated by everything around them; they stare intently at anything new or different. So the goal isn't to make children "color blind." The goal is to change the *importance* kids ascribe to those differences.

The power of the Hilliard and Liben "boys and girls" study is that it shows this is precisely where the words adults use matter.

What we say shapes what kids think and how they feel and behave.

Using words draws our attention. (Ghostbusters, anyone? "Whatever you do, DON'T think of a giant marshmallow man!") The question is, what do you want to draw attention *to*? Does it matter that there are boys and girls? Do you need them to be thinking of that at this moment? If not, don't use the phrase. A simple group word works in its place. A group word is appropriate, in fact, because you *are* addressing the group. There's no need to draw distinctions and create divisions. You want cohesion and unity, and so it's better to use language that supports the development of this concept. "Class" or "children" works very well. "Friends" works well for younger children, especially preschoolers. "Room 7" works if the school uses room numbers. Heck, even "kiddos" is fine.

I realize that the practice of saying "boys and girls" is longstanding. That doesn't make it useful. If you really want to see how nonsensical it is, try this: Take any other equally valid category for your students and use that to address them: "blacks and whites," "freshmen and sophomores," "affluent kids and free- or reduced-lunch kids," "blondes and brunettes."

Clearly, there are times when it makes sense to draw distinctions: "woodwinds and percussion" in a band rehearsal, "kindergartners and first-graders" in a combined classroom, or "anyone who is editing and those who are still writing" in an English class. The point is that distinctions should be drawn when they serve the purpose of education, not just out of habit.

Because what we say shapes how kids think and act. We should choose our words carefully and in principled ways.

"Run Like a Girl" Ad Campaign

Here's one more example of how language shapes our actions, played out over a longer time period.

Have you seen "Run Like a Girl," the 2014 ad campaign run by Always? This video packs a visual punch. I've shown it in many of my classes because it manages to hit topics of child development, cognitive development, play, and creativity.

In the video, we see teens being asked to show what it looks like to "run like a girl." They flop around, look silly, laugh, and generally look pathetic—or at least apathetic. Then the video shows younger girls—importantly, prepuberty aged—being asked the same question. These young girls run full out—unselfconscious and full of vitality. The video goes back to the older girls. Each is asked if she'd like the chance to redo her run. They all do. The teen girls saw the raw power of the younger girls. And you, the viewer, can see in their eyes the recognition of something lost. Why? Why was it lost? When did "run like a girl" become an insult? When did the idea of being a girl become equated with being pathetic?

Again I want to stress this isn't about being politically correct.

This is about understanding that our words teach kids what to think. Parents and teachers who understand this can use that knowledge to speak in ways that align with their goals for kids.

Things to Try

1. When reading picture books to your child, notice the pronouns the author used. Are you surprised?

2. Today, when you are reading aloud, try alternating pronouns. Reflect on how you feel (uncomfortable? happy? ...?).

3. When talking to a prepuberty-aged girl, notice the words you use about girls and girlhood. When talking to a teenaged girl, ask what she likes (and dislikes) about being a girl in society today. Then reflect—where did those ideas come from?

2

Language Development

Wired to learn what we hear

A note before you start. This chapter is more technical than most of the others. I think it really helps people working with children to have a window into language development generally, and I offer this overview to put the rest of the book into context. For readers interested in the science of language development, this chapter is definitely for you! If you prefer to skim (or skip!) this one, **there are two big take-aways I'd like you to know:**

- We are wired for human sound.
- Nothing is more important to a baby or young child than what their parent is doing and saying.

Infant research over the past thirty to forty years has shown very clearly that we are born already wired to pay attention to human voices speaking human language sounds (e.g., Vouloumanos & Werker, 2007). This preference is in place from the moment of birth (e.g., Moon, Cooper & Fifer, 1993). Although hearing will improve over the first ten years, much of the child's auditory capacity is in place from Day One. And while any language is better than neutral tones, newborn infants are shown to prefer listening to their native language(s). We are wired to take it in, learn it, and reproduce it.

Note: I focus here on spoken language because that is the neurotypical route and the most common. It is abundantly clear that full language input can come in via signed languages. More on that later in this chapter.

This chapter drives home the research showing how children are born wired to listen to us. It starts with one big idea central to human language development, plus a couple of key points to understand and keep in mind. I show what the research has found about how infants are wired for human speech sounds and how infants move from understanding sounds to words. I look at the exception of deafness and what research on sign language has shown about spoken language. I introduce the four aspects of human language development (these are explored much more deeply in Chapter 3, "A Deeper Dive") and touch on the social and biological bases for learning to communicate. The chapter closes with a discussion of research on bilingual and multilingual development and how research into digital input shows that we need to use language in order to develop it.

Language Development: One Big Idea and Two Key Points

When I taught language development, I found it helpful to open with one big idea followed by two key points. The big idea is this: **We are wired to learn language by participating in language-using communities.**

Humans are social creatures, born into families in interconnection with others, immersed in the richness of one or more of the 6,900-plus languages spoken on earth. Think about how vulnerable that newborn baby is. They *have* to come to understand us. Their survival and growth depend on it.

Language, fundamentally then, gives us power. In technical terms, language is referred to as a symbol system. The symbol here is not the words themselves, but the fact that we can use sounds as ideas to signify things. With language, we can go beyond pointing or grunting to indicate what we mean. Language enables us to do all kinds of wonderful, powerful things, such as:

- Think and talk about things that aren't present or even real (our trip to the beach, Grandma's visit next month, flying unicorns, becoming a ninja ...)
- Control our thoughts, emotions, and actions
- Affect other people indirectly

In standard academic terms, language is said to *mediate* our experience. It gets in the middle, between us and the world, and it shapes and transforms our experience in that world. This is heady stuff. Babies watch people and see that a lot is achieved through the words people use. As a result, babies are highly motivated to learn the language. In fact, we are so hardwired to learn language that it isn't possible to keep a child from learning whatever language or languages they hear used around them.

That one big idea leads to two key points about language.

- Key Point 1—Comprehension precedes production (learning *what* is easier than learning *how*).
- Key Point 2—Language is a shared accomplishment (it's a two-way street).

Let's look at them in greater detail.

Key Point 1: Comprehension Comes First

This is something that I drilled into my students and which almost universally surprised them. Babies get what we are talking about *long* before they can speak. That means we need to be careful what we say to them, and within their hearing range.

It makes sense if you think about it. Learning *about* something is almost always easier than learning *how to do it*. Think armchair quarterbacks or backseat drivers. Think about all that commentary in the Olympics, the slow-motion video, and cool animations breaking down the intricate moves in gymnastics, or diving, or ski jumping. We can see what they're talking about. We can understand how the move is supposed to work. We surely can't do it though.

It's the same with language development. Babies hear us and start to make sense of what we're saying long before their physical development allows them to control their mouth and vocal chords. **It isn't that babies don't have language, it's that they don't have *speech*.** They have what is known as *communicative intent*—the desire to convey their meaning. And they have it much earlier than they can talk.

Developmental science has proposed this for several decades. Brain science just recently backed it up. In 2014, a study published in the preeminent journal *Proceedings of the National Academy of Sciences* showed that babies were essentially rehearsing language sounds several months before they could speak (Kuhl, et al, 2014). Seven-month-olds were placed into magneto-encephalography machines listening to speech sounds. Brain areas known to be involved in the *motor planning* of speech production lit up as preverbal seven-month-olds *listened* to speech sounds. These babies' brains were processing the sound and preparing for eventual speaking, months before they would be able to produce words. *Comprehension comes before production*.

The other point here is that production is being built long before we see evidence of it. It matters what we do and say.

One caveat though: Comprehension comes first, but it doesn't guarantee production. Speaking the language may or may not follow. Many people are familiar with the phenomenon of knowing a language and not being able to speak it. Living in California, I can understand a great deal of Spanish—but I'm pretty useless at speaking it. Many children of immigrants discover that they can *understand* their parents or grandparents, but they can't *answer* them in the family's native language.

Key Point 2: It Takes Two to Tango

Communication is a shared accomplishment. When babies finally start talking, no one can actually tell what they're saying. They talk funny: they aren't good at articulating sounds. That's because simultaneously controlling all the parts that make speech sounds (the lips, tongue, teeth, cheeks, and vocal chords) takes effort. And babies have to *learn* how to do that.

So babies are very reliant on their caregivers to interpret what that "bankie" or "ba" or "do" is supposed to mean. They combine gestures and expressions with whatever sound they're making; what developmental science calls *holophrases*. People close to the baby **take that holophrase to mean something.** The adults and older children in their lives know a lot about the baby's life and patterns, and the baby's likes and dislikes. Siblings are especially attuned to this. I've known lots of cases where an older sibling could understand a baby when the parent couldn't.

With the idea that the baby *means something*, now we're off to the races. Life changes dramatically in homes at this point. The baby sees that "when I do this, it gets me that." And that kind of association is the fundamental building block of everything we ever learn, especially language.

How We Know Babies Are Wired for Human Speech Sound

As I said at the beginning of this chapter, it is now widely accepted that babies are born wired to attend to human speech. How do we know this? The human propensity for language sounds has been measured both behaviorally and through brain imaging. Behaviorally, researchers have taken advantage of babies' naturally occurring motions in order to tell what a baby prefers. We can track where and how long a baby looks. We can hook babies up to machines that show how much they turn their heads or how much they increase their rate of sucking. In brain science, researchers can measure increases in blood oxygen levels to parts of the brain used for processing language, as well as changes in magnetic fields that indicate thought process.

We now know that from birth:

1. Babies prefer human speech sounds.

2. They prefer the sounds of their native language(s).

3. They can distinguish speech sounds across the full range of human languages.

4. They can discriminate between languages that have very different rhythms. (For a detailed review of this research, I recommend Janet Werker and Judit Gervain's chapter, "Speech Perception," in the 2013 Oxford Handbook of Developmental Psychology as one example.)

Point 3 above has been the subject of a lot of research. It has been clearly shown that babies are born with an ability that we all lose quite early on. From birth, we initially can distinguish any spoken language sound on the planet. Over time, this is lost, or at least modified.

This is a counterintuitive concept—that we would lose abilities we have at birth. But up until about six to eight months of age, all babies react to human speech sound the same way, and by ten to twelve months of age, that has changed. What changes is not about hearing, exactly. It's about perceiving.

Research over the past decades has clearly shown that babies can perceive subtle differences in spoken sounds that older kids and adults miss. It's not that we adults don't hear them; our ears work fine. It's that we don't *perceive* them. What I mean is that we don't detect that they are different from the speech sounds we are accustomed to hearing. We literally don't notice the difference in sound.

How do we know this is different for infants?

The Habituation Technique

Babies can't tell us what they're thinking. On top of that, they are often uncomfortable with strangers, and they get cranky, tired, and hungry. And they certainly won't do what we ask simply to be polite! Because of this, research on infants is typically done using a technique called *habituation*, which takes advantage of a well-known characteristic of babies: they love new things.

Habituation works by offering something—an object or event or sound—to a baby so many times that the baby is no longer interested by it. When they get bored, babies tend to disengage and look away or tune out.

At that point, the baby is offered a new thing and the researcher watches to see how the baby reacts. If they don't really perceive it to be different, they will continue their bored, disengaged behavior. But if the infant takes notice of the new thing, it can be said that they detected the difference. Habituation lets us use the baby's renewed interest as a way of determining what the baby is able to perceive.

Speech Perception Research

In speech perception research, the standard research method is to bring the baby into a darkened sound booth, seated on its mother's lap, and play it sounds to listen to. To train babies to the sound they're interested in, researchers pair that sound with an interesting event; typically, a box off to the side of the infant will light up and some kind of mechanical toy will appear to capture the baby's interest. After the baby has had a chance to enjoy seeing the toy, the light will go off and the toy disappears. The baby will then look away to find something more interesting to look at than a blank, dark box! Babies are quick to notice patterns, and over repeated rounds, they learn to associate that particular sound with the fun toy. This allows the researchers to present different language sounds that are very close. When babies detect the known sound amidst the other language sounds, they respond by turning to see the lit-up toy. By turning, they show us that they can detect the difference between that sound and another one.

What's wild is that researchers have shown that up to about age six to eight months, all infants respond to human language sounds the same way. They can hear small, subtle differences in any variety of languages, even languages they've never heard before. But by the time they are ten to twelve months, babies respond to the sounds of unknown languages just like any adult does. They no longer turn to see the lit-up toy. They simply don't notice small sound distinctions they could easily detect a few months earlier.

This capability led infant language researcher Patricia Kuhl, co-director of the Institute for Learning and Brain Sciences at University of Washington, to call newborn babies "citizens of the world."

If you're intrigued by this, it really helps to hear the process. I recommend Kuhl's excellent TEDx Ranier talk from 2011 and also the website or youTube videos for researcher Janet Werker, who directs the Infant Studies Centre at University of British Columbia. They are two of the foremost researchers on infant language development today, and each has been working in the field for well over twenty years.

Patricia Kuhl uses the phrases "citizens of the world" versus "culture bound listeners" to denote this break point in infant language development. Kuhl argues that babies are "taking statistics" for the first six to eight months, building a neural structure for understanding human speech. In her terms, babies are forming their brain connections for the patterns of their native language or languages. After ten to twelve months, Kuhl argues that infants are drawing from the memory structures they have built in preparation for speaking.

Processing Speech Sounds, Preparing to Speak

We know there is this difference between how a six- to eight-month-old infant perceives language sounds versus how a ten- to twelve-month-old or older infant does. The current research is looking into both the how and the why behind this. It looks as if what's happening is that in those last few months leading up to their first spoken word, babies are attuning themselves to the language or languages that they need to speak.

Recent evidence suggests that's exactly what's happening. Popping babies in the space-age scanning machines mentioned earlier (*magnetoencephalography* or MEG), Kuhl and colleagues have discovered that babies' brains are very busy when they're listening to spoken language. They're busy in precisely the areas that control *motor* movements that produce speech.

When we talk, we don't have to think about it, but there is a lot of physical work going on. The mouth, tongue, teeth, and voice box all need to be recruited in the right ways to make the correct sounds. Certain areas of the brain plan and coordinate those movements, specifically, Broca's area and the cerebellum.

Recall that there are two sides to language development: comprehension and production. Babies have to understand what we're saying, so it's obvious that their brains would be active in the areas for language comprehension. What's news is that before they can speak, babies' brains are *also* busy in the areas for language production as well: actively planning and coordinating the mouth movements needed to produce speech sounds, months before they will say their first word.

Furthermore, Kuhl have shown that babies' brains are processing native and non-native languages differently. At that early window when we know infants perceive all human speech sounds—six to eight months—the MEG shows that infant brains treat any human speech sound equally. At the older window—ten to twelve months—the brain scanners show that the motor planning part of infants' brains has to work harder to process non-native speech sounds.

Babies are learning how to speak. Their *brains* are learning how to speak. What we say to them and around them is what they have available as the rehearsal material— whether it is in English, Arabic, Swahili, or Mandarin.

From Sounds to Words

This baseline of ability from birth is fascinating, and yet it's only part of the work that infants do. An explosion of research over the past fifteen to twenty years has looked at how babies decode human speech sounds. How and when do babies sort out that all these sounds *mean something*?

The problem is immediately apparent if you listen to a foreign language. One playful activity I used when I taught child development drew on the fact that at San Jose State University I could count on there being at least five or six different languages spoken in any given class. I would have a student think of a short sentence to say in a language other than English. They'd say it out loud without translating it for us.

Then I'd ask if anyone who didn't know the language had understood what was said. That was always an easy no.

But then I'd surprise them by asking if anyone knew *how many words* had just been said. Everyone was stumped—and a little stunned to realize that they had no idea. So we would repeat it for a second language, and then a third and a fourth and a fifth. It was both fun and illuminating because the students saw that they don't get any better—it's just wild guessing every time. When hearing a new language, we simply have no idea how to break the stream of sound apart into chunks of sounds that correspond to words.

And that's the beauty of the activity—because that's exactly what babies have to do. They take the stream of sound coming across their ears, and they slowly determine which sounds fall together and where the breaks between sounds are. It takes months of listening for them to be able do this. And if they are growing up in a bilingual or multilingual home, they are doing this across two or more languages. Babies are essentially squishy pattern recognition machines. They listen and they learn.

But remember the big idea: we are hardwired to learn language **by participating in language-using communities.** Babies are able to work with these sounds from their native language or languages *when they hear them in the context of everyday activity.* They slowly pattern the sounds they hear to the actions and objects they see. They slowly untangle the stream of sound into little packets of sound bites that conform to words, and also slowly uncover the meaning those words have. It's an amazing accomplishment, which virtually each and every living human being does effortlessly.

In the background of this human process is the question of *what* words the baby is hearing. The thrust of this book is to understand *how* what we say structures what children understand. We have to see first that whatever they hear will go in. And it does. Usually.

Except When We Don't

To see why this is so important, we need to look at what happens when things go wrong: what happens when babies don't get language input?

There is a myriad of gripping stories of children raised in the wild, discovered, and "domesticated." Or of children found in deplorable conditions, deprived of human contact. Invariably, these children do not develop full adult levels of language use. The Wild Boy of Aveyron and Genie are the two cases most intro psychology students will recognize, though their circumstances differed profoundly. What such atypical development cases have illuminated is **the extent to which human language capacity develops only in the midst of active language use.**

These dramatic stories of children raised by wolves, or in forests, or even grotesquely abused in quiet suburban communities never fail to captivate public interest. But there are actually many more mundane instances that make the point equally well: deaf children born to hearing parents.

Fascinating research with deaf children has led to the understanding that humans are wired for language input *even if they can't hear*. Language input comes most commonly as speech. But in the case of deaf children, that channel is simply not available. Most families, when they figure out that their child is not hearing them, seek medical attention and school support for them. These children can and do grow up to lead full and healthy lives. Case in point: in 2013, Harvard Law School graduated the first deafblind lawyer, Haben Girma. Not hearing is not a barrier to a great life.

If parents do not recognize that their child is not hearing them, though, deaf children are indeed at risk of not developing their full language potential/capacity. Recent instances of sign-language development speak to this. In Nicaragua in 1977, a group of deaf children were housed together for the first time, creating a sort of institution for them. Since no such accommodations had existed, the children arrived with disparate homesign vocabularies they had worked out with their individual families. Remember: babies have communicative intent. They and the families who love them work hard to make sense of their desires.

In some cases, children had very limited signs, and in others, children arrived with complex sets of signs. One problem arose immediately. These individual signs largely did not overlap. The children had to work together to make themselves understood.

As these things go, once there was a place for housing deaf children, more were brought there. Over the next few years, hundreds more children were brought to the center. The "school" population grew, and younger children arrived. Over time, the youngest children adopted the shared sign use quickly and developed it more and more fully. The community of deaf children living together literally created a new language. Nicaraguan Sign Language (NSL) has been well studied, and it is now considered by linguists to be a full language. It emerged as a result of the children being brought together and being motivated to understand one another—all in the absence of hearing any language spoken. The children who arrived first, however, do not speak it fully, or fluently.

A similar trend has been seen in Israel over the past eighty years. A 2016 news article from the preeminent research journal *Science* outlines current research into the development of Israeli Sign Language (ISL). Linguists studying the development of ISL showed that each subsequent generation of signers refined and added complexity to the language. This research affirms both the big idea that language development requires social interaction as well as the two key points about comprehension and other people.

What the research on these and other sign languages shows us is that 1) the desire to communicate is innate—families find ways of communicating around the sound barrier, and 2) the ability to learn language requires full language input. (If you are interested in more on this topic, see Diane Brentari and Marie Coppola's 2012 *WIRES* paper, "What Sign Language Creation Teaches Us About Language.")

Children, then, are born into their families already wired to develop a desire to communicate. Neurotypical hearing children will do that by absorbing and internalizing whatever language or languages they hear. It is a small step to seeing, then, that what we say to kids shapes what they will understand about the world.

Four Aspects of Language Development

So we're wired to listen, to learn what we hear, and to put that together to communicate with those around us. To do this, there are four aspects that build together to give us spoken language:

1. Sound, or *phonology*. The sounds of each human language are unique patterns of noises.
2. Meaning, or *semantics*. The meaning of the language is what we ascribe to those sounds. The sound "trub" might not mean anything to us, but the sounds "tree" and "l'arbre" actually refer to something.
3. Grammar. The particular rules for combining words into sentences. (It's the only aspect that uses its colloquial term.)
4. Communication, or *pragmatics*. The intent behind the use of words with other people. It packages the first three into a bundle for actual use.

Let me explain briefly what each aspect means.

The Sounds of the Language (Phonology)

Human speech is marvelous. All over the world, people have developed languages that use soft sounds and hard sounds, clicks, gurgles, guttural sounds, and tones. Far from random noise, human speech is organized, highly structured, and must follow a particular sequence in order for another speaker to fully understand what is being said.

Babies are born into a social environment where one or more human languages are spoken by the people who surround them. They must hear and differentiate these sounds in order to be able to become fluent speakers.

The Meaning of the Words (Semantics)

We package sounds into little packets of meaning. Just look at the word *sentence*. The sound *sen* means nothing, *t* by itself means nothing, and the sound *ence* means nothing. But we have come to agree that the string of sounds *sentence* has a meaning. It's like this with every word we speak, in every language spoken.

Babies have to learn first that this game is happening. Then on top of that, they have to learn the meanings of the words they hear. It goes without saying that if you are not exposed to a word, you can't learn it. What we hear, and later what we read, comprises our vocabulary.

The Grammar of the Language

Whatever else you think of grammar, it has a technical definition: it is the set of rules for combining words into sentences. Languages vary as to where the words are allowed to fall: adjectives before the noun (blue ball) or after (*le bal bleu*); verbs before the subject (they want to kick the ball) or at the end of the sentence (*sie wollen den Ball zu treton*).

Children learn the grammar of their native language or languages innately. If you've travelled to a place where a different language is spoken, you may have had the experience of getting your meaning across. We can get by pretty well in broken whatever (English, Spanish, Turkish, etc). Yet children are driven to learn the grammar, and even without being corrected by adults, they will self-correct over time. (It's another issue altogether with written language; that has to be taught in all but rare cases).

Communicating with Others (Pragmatics)

All of the previous three aspects of language development combine to serve the ability to use words to communicate our thoughts and desires to others. Our ability to use language effectively is based on more than just our vocabulary and being able to make nice-sounding sentences. We also have to understand how to use our words to achieve actions and to understand how others will interpret what we say. This is complex stuff, and it takes us years to fully develop an understanding of the nuances of language use.

(In the next chapter, I discuss each of these four aspects of language development in greater depth, drawing on research with infants and children to show how the language they hear shapes what they think.)

Language *Is* Socialization

At its foundation, I suggest that language *is* socialization. That's a fairly bold statement. Here's why. Children are learning the language or languages native to their family and community just by participating within them. How does that work?

Social Basis for Learning

From the time they're born, children are immersed in social activity and surrounded by adults and other children or youth who are speaking language. Attitudes and mores are transferred from one generation to the next, or from peer to peer, on the wave of the words we choose.

Developmental science has identified three primary ways that children take on the culture they inhabit, and language is the bedrock of all three:

* *Social Enhancement*—Exploring the stuff of the culture. Children have access to it, pick it up, and use it—whether it's physical, like Mom's smartphone, or intangible, like big brother's favorite YouTube video. Language is embedded in all of it—in the artifact itself and in what children hear us say about it.

* *Modeling/Imitation*—Doing what the big people do. Babies have been shown to imitate from as early as six weeks of age, and what they are happiest and most likely to imitate are vocalizations and facial expressions. Increasingly over time, copying others includes talking like them. We speak like our families, we talk like our teachers, and we sound like our friends.

* *Direct Instruction*—Being told what to do and believe. Adults instruct children all the time on how to do specific tasks or to instill general beliefs and behaviors. While nonverbal demonstration may be a component of such teaching, most instruction is done expressly through the use of language.

With these three processes, children are enculturated or socialized into the environment they inhabit. None of these three can happen fully without language. Without language, it would be impossible to know what the tool left lying out was for, or to know the deeper meaning of what we are copying, and certainly to understand the how and why of the way things are done.

Biological Basis for Learning to Communicate

In order to learn from others, we have to be able to attend to and understand them. Again, developmental science has identified a core set of processes that all humans develop. These processes enable us to be in coordination with others and thus to learn from them. They include the following:

* *Attending to Others*—As I've pointed to already, from the moment they're born, babies are wired to seek and pay attention to the people in their environment. Babies' hearing is good from the get-go, and they're oriented to human voices speaking speech sounds. Their vision is not great at birth, but they can lock in on the face of whoever feeds them, and over the first four months, their visual system develops rapidly. By four to four-and-a-half months, they have full visual acuity and depth perception. And they aren't even sitting up yet.

* *Sharing Attention with Others*—Babies *love* being in interaction with other people. They want to share emotional contact and interaction. They nuzzle and smile, they coo, and they do everything they can to draw us to them. Sharing closeness, and feelings, is an important precursor to being able to share language—a prep stage, if you will. Embedded in this intimate sharing is the foundation of turn taking. I smile, you smile. I coo, you coo. This kind of back and forth in physical interaction sets the stage for children's ability to take turns in speech as well.

Beyond sharing emotions, babies learn to share a common focus outside their bodies too. By about nine months of age, babies learn that our gaze is where our attention is. They can look at something with us, and delight in sharing that focus with another person. Babies even recruit our attention! If they want you, babies will vocalize (crying, cooing), or make a noise (jiggle a toy, bang on a table), or my personal favorite, grab your face and turn you to look where they want you to! This ability is called *joint attention*. A shared focus becomes a big part of how parents cue babies to new words, so it's a huge part of vocabulary growth.

Perhaps the biggest child development question I have is what's happening to babies whose caregivers are stuck in their smartphones. We're in the midst of the largest social experiment of all time, launched in 2007 with the first smartphone. Frankly, I'm worried. It troubles me to see a parent nose down in the white glow of their phone as their baby explores the world at their feet, essentially alone while the parent is within arm's reach.

* *Understanding with Others*—Being able to work with and learn from others depends on language. The ability to come to a shared understanding with others—to know what they mean— is what enables us to build our understanding of the world. This ability is called *intersubjectivity,* and it relies on both joint attention AND communication. Only through our words can we fully apprehend what someone else is thinking. Nonverbal methods can convey a ton of meaning—dance, mime, even charades reveal and communicate great depths. But they are also more open to interpretation than words. Even words require interpretation, but their use is nonetheless more direct.

Humans create and maintain language-rich cultures that children are born into and must take part in. Language, then, is the water that socialization into the culture flows in. Children will imitate, explore, and learn from their families and culture via language. How does that language shape how they think?

Bilingualism or Multilingualism

The simplest layer in how language shapes what we think is *which* particular language (or languages) the child learns. Obviously, if you don't hear Korean growing up, you aren't likely to speak it. Children, though, will take in *any* human language they hear used while they're young.

Currently, more than half of the human population speaks two or more languages. I'm frustrated that in the United States the misplaced belief persists that learning a second language will hurt a child. How could it possibly be a disadvantage if half of all people on the planet do it? Separate from a discussion of bilingual education (which has many variations and definite good and negative points) I want to stress that the mere fact of learning two languages at the same time doesn't mess kids up.

In fact, there are increasingly well-documented *cognitive* advantages to speaking two or more languages. There has been a burst of research showing that bilingual children are better able to inhibit conflicting information than are monolingual children, in both visual and spatial tasks. This cognitive control shows up in any task requiring attention and may give bilingual children a leg up in classroom work. Bilingual and multilingual children are also found to have the edge over monolingual children in understanding other people's minds earlier (called *Theory of Mind*). And there is also evidence to suggest that learning two or more languages in infancy or early childhood helps children better understand the uses of language and be more reflective on the aspects of language. (For more detail see, for example, the 2012 comprehensive review of research by Nameera Akhtar and Jennifer Menjivar, in the book *Advances in Child Development and Behavior*.)

There are also huge (and somewhat obvious) social advantages of learning more than one language: being able to connect with more people, especially when that includes family; being able to connect with family heritage; being able to travel easily in different parts of the world; and increasingly, being able to work in a global, hyperconnected world.

Humans are endlessly adaptive. We've had to be to get this far. And kids will soak up whatever language or languages they hear used around them. To date, there is only one documented disadvantage that bilingual and multilingual people experience: they may have a smaller vocabulary within each language than a typical monolingual speaker. Makes sense, doesn't it? If you're learning multiple languages, you might lack the time to learn as many words in each one. It's a cost I think is worth bearing though, given the enormous social and cognitive gains.

In fact, you can't *keep* a kid from learning their native languages. Parents around the globe sometimes drop their voice and speak in a different language to hide what they're saying from their children. Children around the globe hear that cue and strain to listen—knowing that whatever is being said must be pretty juicy. Does using a different language for "grown-up" discussions work? According to my undergraduates, not so much. *Many* of my students shared that they and their siblings had figured out how to understand what their parents were whispering about—and that their parents never knew!

A word to the wise: kids really are listening. And nothing could be more interesting to them than what you are saying. Keep in mind Key Point 1 though, that comprehension is going to precede production. If they hear it, they will learn to understand it. But just hearing the language doesn't guarantee that children will also learn to *speak* it.

Engaging in Language Versus Just Overhearing It

Remember that big idea about how we learn language? **We are wired to learn language by participating in language-using communities.** That means we need to *hear* it spoken and to *answer* in it as well. Many, many children of immigrants have had the experience of growing up understanding what their parents and grandparents are saying in the family's native language, but never using that language themselves. Instead, the children adopt the language of their new country—answering, for example, in English if the family emigrated to the United States or in French if the family moved to France. These children hear their family's native language at home but grow up without practicing speaking it. Like most aspects of life, families just find a way to make this work.

I saw this firsthand when I was a kid. My sister fell in love with her husband when we lived in Australia. He is first-generation Australian-Italian. Like many of my first-generation American students at SJSU, my brother-in-law's family was a close-knit family. Grandparents, aunties, and uncles lived in the homes with the new Australian generation. Despite the fact that his grandparents spoke not a word of English and lived with him, my brother-in-law isn't fluent in Italian.

If you haven't experienced it, you might wonder how that's even possible. But the fact that we're wired to listen to human voices speaking human language sounds isn't enough. We have to participate in life by *using* that language to learn it fully.

What About Digital Input?

This point is particularly relevant to the educational toy market. Starting in the 1990s, notably with the Baby Einstein product line, companies have capitalized on parent concern by marketing edutainment reported to tap into babies' innate language perception abilities. But there's a problem here. Does it matter if the language is being spoken by real people or on television/DVD? Yes, it does. *At least for infants.*

The most impressive research I've seen on this subject comes from Patricia Kuhl and her colleagues (e.g., Kuhl, Tsao, & Liu 2003). Kuhl has shown definitively that babies do not learn foreign language by watching television. But they can learn it quite easily from only a few hours of live interaction. That's what we're wired for.

In her lab, Kuhl had babies do one of three things: listen to audio of another language, watch DVDs of the language, or interact with a researcher speaking that language. These were native English speakers listening to Mandarin. When they were compared later to other monolingual children, only the babies who had interacted with a real live human showed any difference in their ability to notice the unique sounds of Mandarin.

Babies are listening to the distribution of sounds. Remember what I said earlier: they are squishy little pattern recognition machines. As Kuhl puts it, they are "taking statistics" of the sound patterns in the language. Kuhl's distinct point across much of her research is that the social brain controls *when* we take these statistics. Babies' brains are activated when they are engaged with others. That social engagement seems to turn on the brain's learning mechanism.

So—save your money on the Baby Einstein videos. The only way a baby is going to learn another language is by interacting with someone speaking it.

I will say that, at this point, we don't know to what extent interactive tech can replace speaking in person, so e-readers, Skype, and FaceTiming, for example, are wide open areas for research in bilingual development. Interestingly, the American Academy of Pediatricians (AAP) took this into account when they revised their technology recommendations in the fall of 2016.

The AAP is the national organization that represents the nation's children's doctors. Their recommendations are based on medical and psychological research and are intended to guide parents in making the best choices for their children.

Previously—much to the disbelief of my students—the AAP recommendation for screen time was *0* for infants up to age two years. That's right: none. Obviously, that's hard to imagine in today's smartphone-permeated world. Yet the 2016 revision managed both a strong stance and an awareness of the potential for interactive media. In the eight-page policy statement, the AAP outlines the current state of research. The statement closes with recommendations for pediatricians, families, and the media industry. Their leading recommendation to families: "Avoid digital media use (except video chatting) in children younger than eighteen to twenty-four months."

While we know that babies don't learn language from screen media, there are interesting open questions about whether and to what extent young children (preschool age and older) might be able to learn another language from passive media like DVDs.

Certainly some vocabulary is possible, as anyone who's watched a kid watching *Dora the Explorer* knows. And PBS isn't the only group offering foreign language to preschool-aged children. In fact, foreign language software and programming has existed for decades. Rosetta Stone is probably still the gold standard, though there are many other brands. When my children were little, we discovered a series called *Muzzy* through our public library. Produced by the British Broadcasting Corp (BBC), it's been in use for twenty-five years. The website uses all the right keywords to indicate it's based on sound research, but there is no evidence of research to back up their claims that kids actually learn language. (The same was true for Baby Einstein, I might add—right up until the FCC shut them down for fraud).

It is clear that media can support language development in adults, but much less is known about the impact on children. Full language fluency from watching screens seems harder to document or attain. I do think that future (and even near-future) technology offers intriguing possibilities. I will be very interested to see what comes from the newest wave of interactive language software, such as DuoLingo and Google Translate. I also imagine that voice-activated ubiquitous computing and Augmented Reality-Virtual Reality (AR/VR) will offer us enormous new lessons about the limits of human language development.

3

Language Development Research

A deeper dive

With this new understanding that what we say to kids is going in and shaping what they think, it's time to look at the research on how that happens. In this chapter, I take us on a deeper dive into each of the four aspects of language development introduced in Chapter 2: sound, meaning, grammar, and communication. Here, I discuss each aspect more fully, along with intriguing new research showing how intimately children's language capacity is built from the people around them. I start, though, with a quick note about how babies pay attention and how they develop the surprising ability to mask whether they're attending to us.

Note that this is the second of three research-intensive chapters in the book. If you are intrigued by the science of language development, I think this will be a fun read. If you prefer, you might read ahead and return to this chapter when ideas later in the book make you curious about how all this works. For now, please keep in mind three things:

- Babies are attending to us from the moment they are born.
- This is happening even when we don't realize or can't tell.
- Our words are going in, shaping what kids think.

Selective Attention

Babies are wired to pay attention to other human beings from the moment they're born. It's how they survive and how they adapt and learn. This has been demonstrated in research on infant hearing, vision, and even scent. Babies not only have use of their senses when they're born, but they've also been shown to have *preferences*—as soon as nine *minutes* after birth!

Research on infant vision from the 1960s showed us that babies have a preference for human faces, and they have it early—by the time they are two *days* old. Since then, we have learned much more about infants' early visual abilities. Babies are good at tracking human faces while they move, which makes sense since that's what they're likely to see in the real world outside a laboratory. A preference for anything that looks like a face has been measured as early as fifty-three *minutes* after birth. And as we might expect, infants have a preference for whose face they look at—their mother's face has been measured as preferable to infants within two to seven *hours* after birth.

So we know that babies are watching us. We also know they're listening.

As I indicated at the start of Chapter 2, babies are born with a preference for human voices speaking human language sounds. We know from current research that very early on, infants also develop a preference for the sounds of their own native language or languages. This preference becomes more marked as the baby approaches the point of speaking, at about age one.

So it is surprising to learn how early babies can *mask* this interest. And that's important for caregivers to understand.

I routinely stressed to my students that *beginning in infancy*, humans can do what is called *selective attention*. It was easy to demonstrate this in class. I would sit on the edge of a table and face one of the back rows of students. Then I'd ask the class whom they thought I was looking at. Humans are *very* good at reading attention—it was completely clear to the entire class which student I appeared to be paying attention to. So they all were more than a little surprised when—without moving my gaze or position—I started describing in detail what a student off to my left or right had been doing while I was supposedly looking at someone else.

That's selective attention. My students got it with this quick demo. And they were stunned to learn that babies can do it as early as four months of age!

This is important to understand. Because **starting at four months of age,** when the baby appears to be paying attention to a toy, or the television, or something in the other room, **chances are very good that in fact they're paying attention to every word you're saying.**

This has big implications for their language development. What we say is highly important and interesting to children. As previously mentioned, they are tuned to it even when we think they're not. Try dropping your voice when the kids are in another room. Then say something like "cookie" or the child's name, and you'll see that they are indeed listening!

Phonology Research with Children

For hearing babies learning spoken language, there are two sides of the "sound" coin: interpreting the incoming sounds (*comprehension*) and learning to make them (*production*).

The idea that these are separate processes is strong in psychology. It's bizarre to me though. How could they possibly be separate? Anyone learning to speak a language is obviously doing it from the input they get—whether that is spoken, written, via video, or signed. With new brain-imaging technologies, we're starting to see that our brain processes are far more interconnected than we previously understood.

In a 2015 study published in the *Proceedings of the National Academy of Sciences*, the research world got a wake-up call that these processes are not as separate as psychologists had managed to convince themselves. It turns out babies move their tongue and practice a sound as they hear it, in order to learn it. Keep them from being able to move their tongue, and you keep them from being able to learn the sound!

Internationally acclaimed infant language researcher Janet Werker and her colleagues, led by Alison Bruderer, designed a simple but conclusive study to see how the ability to produce speech might be connected to the ability to detect it.

In this research, six-month-old babies were brought into a lab and put through a speech perception test like the one I described earlier, where babies listen to speech sounds so researchers can see if they perceive the difference. Science builds in very small steps. Once an area is tested and understood, new explorations can be added on top of that. So using this well-established technique, researchers were able to ask a new question: what are babies doing with their tongues as they're hearing speech?

If you've raised kids or worked with infants, you know that they're not going to just let you peer into their mouth. So these researchers designed a clever workaround: they gave babies something to put in their mouths and then looked to see if that interfered with what the babies were *hearing*.

Recall that between six and eight months, all babies would be expected to detect the differences in speech sounds. The six-month-old babies in this study were given teething toys to chew on while they listened to speech sounds. Some were normal teething toys. Others were designed to obstruct the baby's tongue from moving—particularly the way it would need to move *in order to make that same sound*.

What they found was pretty cool. Plain teething toys didn't interfere. Babies performed just as expected, responding to the new speech sound. But teething toys that blocked the tongue *did* interfere. They prevented the baby from recognizing or learning the new speech sound. Fascinating.

I share this because it reinforces two things I think are important to keep in mind as you go through this book:

1. Babies learn language(s) by being engaged in socially shared, communal language use.
2. Babies are literally rehearsing the words we say from the time they can sit up on their own (possibly sooner).

They are learning what we say. What we say to them matters. Let's take a deeper look at both sides of that speech sound coin.

Interpreting Speech Sounds

As I mentioned previously, human speech is highly structured. There are acceptable sequences to how the sounds fit together, and these can be learned. A baby's job is to hear and differentiate these sounds in order to be able to become a fluent speaker.

Babies learn to segment the language in truly intricate ways. There are some fascinating research findings on how they do it.

Looking at a Speaker's Lips

Babies look at whoever is talking to them. The idea that seeing the speaker *helps them* accurately interpret what is being said was news awhile back. When I was in grad school in 1995, one of the faculty talked about his research on speech perception. It was groundbreaking stuff, using computer models of human speaking. They were able to show that facial information is a big part of what is processed in order to understand speech. But Dom Massaro's team wasn't particularly interested in children or infants. They weren't looking at how speech perception developed or how babies learn to interpret speech. They were chasing the more general question of how facial features were used and particularly how that information was integrated.

What struck me then was the realization that there must be so much more going on than we take for granted. If babies are looking at our mouths when we talk in order to understand what we say, what else are they doing?

Research into infants' use of the speaker's lips has continued. One of the key researchers in this field today is David Lewkowicz, a developmental psychologist at Florida Atlantic University. A 2012 study published in the *Proceedings of the National Academy of Sciences* showed that babies who are listening to a person speaking will shift their attention at particular ages.

Lewkowicz and his grad student Amy Hansen-Tift identified a progression: four-month-olds look at the speaker's eyes, six-month-olds split their attention between the eyes and the mouth, and both eight- and ten-month-olds attend primarily to the speaker's mouth. At twelve months of age—the same age at which most infants will produce their first spoken word—babies shift their attention back to the eyes of the person speaking.

The researchers think that as infants are building the capacity to speak, they focus on the shape of the mouth as a way to learn *how* to make the speech sounds. Once that is in place, though, they can return their focus to the speaker's *eyes*—a more natural source of information about the conversation itself.

Lewkowicz has also shown that bilingual (and presumably multilingual) babies have a different progression to this strategy. Bilingual babies start leveraging the double input of eyes and mouth, what researchers call *redundant audiovisual speech cues,* at a younger age, and they continue for a longer period of time. It makes sense. This strategy helps disambiguate unfamiliar speech sounds. Monolingual babies hearing a foreign language at twelve months shift their gaze/attention to the speaker's mouth. Even adults who can't quite make out what a person is saying will unconsciously gaze at the person's mouth. There's even a well-supported study technique based on this idea, which I've often given my students: if you're having difficulty understanding the material, look at the instructor's mouth as they speak.

It seems that bilingual kids are in on this strategy earlier than monolingual kids. More recently, Lewkowicz and his colleagues have shown that bilinguals are already splitting their attention between eyes and mouth at four months—a full two months earlier than monolingual babies. That's a third of their life at that point! A 2015 study led by Ferran Pons and published in *Psychological Science* found that at eight months, like monolinguals, bilingual babies look more at the mouth than the eyes. But bilinguals continue to do so up to twelve months, when monolingual peers have returned to gazing at the speaker's eyes.

Differentiating Lip Patterns for Foreign Language

A 2007 study led by Whitney Weikum, a graduate student in Janet Werker's infant language perception lab, and published in the journal *Science*, showed that babies could tell when a speaker switched languages—even when they couldn't hear what was being said! In the experiment, infants watched a video of a woman speaking either English or French, with the sound turned off. At four and six months of age, all babies behaved the same way: they perked up when the actor changed languages and watched with renewed interest—even though they couldn't hear what the speaker was saying. At eight months of age, though, only the bilingual babies continued this behavior. The monolingual babies seemed not to notice. As with Lewkowicz's research above, the bilingual babies appeared to be differentially aware of the speaker's mouth patterns, which would make sense given that they experience competing verbal input.

All of this is to say that babies—whether single language or dual language learners—are doing a tremendous amount of work to attend to us. Babies are wired to figure out what we are saying, so that they can learn how to say it too. They are going to pick up everything we say and use that to learn the language. The words we use around them form the foundation of their understanding.

Producing Speech Sounds

There's a joke that parents spend the first year of their child's life dying for them to start talking—and the next seventeen wanting them to be quiet!

Babies typically speak their first true word at around twelve months of age, but of course they make *sounds* from the moment of birth. There's a progression in how humans learn to make the sounds for speech, and it is one of the best-mapped pieces of child developmental science. A quick summary here will help.

Developmental Trajectory of Speech Production

Crying. Babies start at birth with crying. It's all they have to use that first month, and they work it. They have to. It's a survival adaptation, given the utter helplessness with which they arrive.

Cooing. At about one month, babies start to explore their ability to make sounds, first with vowel sounds, which are the easiest. We make vowels by shaping our mouths and closing off the vocal chords. Try this—go from *aayy* to *aahh* to *eeee* to *oooo* and notice what's changing inside you. Place your fingertips on your vocal chords and try it again. Babies discover this and enjoy playing with it, testing it out, producing gleeful cooing sounds.

Articulating. At about three months, babies extend the vowel cooing to making consonant noises. Consonants are made when we get our lips, tongue, and teeth involved (gums for babies). Again, I encourage you to actually try this—*ttttt* to *mmmm* to *pppp* to *lllll*—and feel how the different parts of your mouth are utilized for speech sounds. Despite learning to do it long ago, most of us have never thought about it before.

Babies work with the consonants as single sounds, exploring them for a few months. They're not talking. They're just playing.

Babbling. Around six months, babies extend their range by starting to combine the two kinds of sounds. Consonants and vowels together form the basis of human speech, and so it starts to sound as if they might be talking. This phase is called *babbling,* though, because it isn't coherent or meaningful.

Many parents take these earlier sounds—especially the "mama" or "papa" sounds—to be first words. That is why so many languages have developed so that the words for parents map onto early babbling sounds: *mama, dada, papa, oma, eba,* etc.

Jargoning. Around eight or nine months, babies advance again and start stringing their babbling sounds into vocal patterns that sound like sentences. They've been listening to their native language or languages for months now, and they are showing that they've got the tonal pattern down. They sound like fluent speakers with the ups and downs unique to whatever language(s) they're learning—and yet it's complete gibberish. (For a fantastic example, see the gibberish videos on YouTube.)

Talking! At about their first birthday, on average, babies speak their first true word. This is when they match a sound to a meaning and use it to try to communicate something to someone else. This opens their world up in a big way.

A lot of parents and caregivers don't realize the extent to which babies are listening long before the point when the baby is speaking. My students' single most frequent comment was that they had no idea babies were paying attention that early. They realized that they and their families really only started thinking about what the baby heard once the baby was talking.

Keep in mind: what you say is going in from the very early days. It is shaping what the baby understands and believes. Let's look now at how they start to interpret the words themselves.

Semantics Research with Children

For a sound to be a word, it has to be used to *mean* something. How do children learn that?

There is some debate about babies' word understanding prior to six months. Researchers differ on how much of a baby's ability to interact with us is based on actually understanding the meaning of the words versus merely recognizing the patterns of sounds coupled with familiar interactions. Beyond six months though, researchers agree that children are building word knowledge. And babies have been shown to use single word signs as early as six months.

One current conjecture among early childhood educators is that some (or much) of the tantrumming during the terrible twos stems from the frustration of not being able to make themselves understood. That would do it for me, certainly. I'm always floored at physicist Stephen Hawking's level of perseverance. Imagine having that much to say and not being able to get it out easily—or at all.

Baby sign language has become popular with parents in the past fifteen to twenty years, based largely on research in the 1980s and 1990s that found babies can use signs to indicate what they want up to six months before they can produce a spoken word. I was intrigued enough by the research to try signing with my own two kids and found that they both produced signs—lots of them—before speaking much. With no control group (I couldn't raise two other babies in a box), I can't say if it actually decreased their tantrums, but it was fun for them and me and it did seem to help them communicate. As hearing children of hearing parents, once their spoken language development kicked in though, it quickly outstripped the signing, which ultimately faded entirely.

We know that babies typically produce their first spoken word at about their first birthday. Another way to think about this is that it takes about twelve months of listening and learning before they say their first true word. And keep in mind that they have *communicative intent* months before that.

Vocabulary Development

We go from being able to say that one word around our first birthday to somewhere between 60,000-100,000 words as adults.

There are different takes on the precise rate of word acquisition. Across textbooks on language development, there is general agreement on these points though: following that first spoken word, babies add new vocabulary slowly at first, and then more rapidly. At eighteen months, they may have a spoken vocabulary of about fifty words, and at thirty months, that's likely to be around five hundred words. Age six will see on average around six thousand words spoken, and by the end of high school, perhaps around fifty thousand. How do we get there?

A famous study by Susan Carey back in 1978 led to an idea in language development called *fast mapping*. Eighteen-month-olds in a preschool were introduced to a new word for a color. The teacher used it on one occasion, asking the children in the study to get the "chromium" tray or the "chromium" cup from next to the red one. Trays were familiar to the toddlers. Cups were too. The red tray and red cup were familiar to them. So these little eighteen-month-olds quickly discerned that their teacher's weird new word must go with the tray or cup they'd never seen before. That is, they mapped the new word *sound* to a physical *thing* in the classroom.

The researchers then waited a week and retested the toddlers' response to the word *chromium*. About two-thirds of the toddlers used the term correctly. When the researchers came back six weeks after the study, many toddlers still knew what color chromium was. One use, and it was locked in. Hence the term *fast mapping*. Kids use what they know about their environment and us to lock on to the meaning of new words.

A rapidly expanding vocabulary is a normal, predictable part of human language development. There's no need to buy vocab-building DVDs for toddlers; they won't learn more from them. In fact, they're better off with face-to-face interaction and maybe some books.

But back to Key Point 1 for a moment: Comprehension precedes production. What children can *say* is far less than what they *understand*. That's because recognizing a word requires only having the memory of it and retrieving that memory. Speaking a word requires much more: having the memory of the word, retrieving it when the context is appropriate, and coordinating all the neurophysiology for controlling the vocal chords and mouth to create the right sounds. It's a lot of work to talk!

So just how much smaller is a child's spoken vocabulary compared to what they understand? About *ten times less*, at least in the early years! A fourteen-month-old toddler who can say about ten different words? It's a safe bet she *understands* about a hundred different words. And that two-year-old who may still be saying little two-word "sentences" made from a few hundred words? She probably understands the meaning of closer to three thousand! This differential between what is understood versus what gets said persists through childhood but decreases over time. Consider that even adults tend to know more words than they typically use.

Morphemes: The Stuff of Language

A relevant term to introduce here is *morpheme*. A *morpheme* is the smallest unit of meaning. I used to show my students that the word *morpheme* has two parts: *morph* and *eme*. *Morph* has to do with form: *morphing* something changes its appearance. The *eme* part is an ending used in linguistics.

Word meaning gets carried by the morphemes. Teaching in California most of my students understand some Spanish, and know that *ito* means *little*. For example, Juanito is Juan's son. Trader Joe's grocery used this morpheme when they invented a word for a new appetizer. My students easily guessed that *tamalitos* were little tamales!

Another example is the ending *-let*. We know that baby pigs are piglets. Baby eagles are eaglets. Asked to name a baby tree, three-year-olds might call it a treelet. It's not a real word, but we know what they mean. That's the morpheme at work. Young children hear these little sub-units of words. And they use them to learn what new words mean.

The Importance of Interaction for Word Learning

In the Phonology section we saw that babies use a speaker's lips to learn new words. I suspect this is part of why videos and apps don't help babies and young children. Interaction that's face-to-face—playful, close, and affectionate—cues the infant brain to, as Patricia Kuhl puts it, "take statistics." A DVD may get their attention, but have you ever seen a baby staring at a screen glassy-eyed? Just because they're looking doesn't mean they're learning from it. So how do babies learn new words?

Early on, babies and toddlers imitate our actions. They see the *intention* guiding our behavior, and they use that to try to master the physical world. They do this with language too. In eighteen short months on the planet, babies figure out that where we look is where our interest is—so the things we talk about are probably whatever we're attending to. Combine this with the fact that babies prefer to be in interaction with people, and the best thing we could do for their vocabulary development is to play with them, talk to them, and read to them.

You may have heard about the "word gap" or the "thirty-million word gap." This term arises from a 1995 study by Betty Hart and Todd Risley, which found that low-income, low-education parents spoke considerably less to their preschoolers than did higher-educated, higher-income parents. The thirty-million word finding is popular in the press, but no one has replicated the Hart and Risley study and there are deep concerns about the methodology. Recent research has confirmed, though, that children from low socioeconomic (SES) families are indeed at a disadvantage. Stanford psychologist Anne Fernald and colleagues in a 2012 study published in *Developmental Science* showed that by the tender age of eighteen months, low-SES children were already six months behind their high-SES peers in both vocabulary development and language processing speed.

Setting aside the exact numbers for a moment, it does appear that lower-income, lower-educated parents speak less with their children. It is certainly the case that these children arrive at school with a smaller working vocabulary and less exposure to school-related words. If you add in a home language other than English, it's easy to see that many low-SES children start school at a disadvantage. Which is why school readiness programs for low-income children include vocabulary exposure.

All this research on semantic development boils down to a simple recommendation: kids need us to interact with them.

Grammar Research with Children

Children around the world learn to speak their native language or languages fluently. They do this with remarkable ease. And they do it regardless of whether they are corrected in the proper way to speak and even if they don't go to school.

Human beings are motivated to learn their native language(s) and to speak them correctly. To do this, we internalize the grammar of the language. Grammar is simply the set of rules a language uses to order words into sentences. Languages vary in how this is done, though there are language families that share similar rules. By and large, adult speakers achieve the same fluent level of speech.

A colleague shared a story that makes this point. Born in Italy to American parents, his family returned to the States when he was ten. He didn't use his Italian much, but when the chance to travel to Italy at age fifty came up, he was eager to return. He found his Italian came back to him easily, and delighted in using it everywhere he went. He noticed, though, that people were looking at him oddly. And that many started speaking really, really slowly. He considered that maybe his accent wasn't as good as he'd thought, but a friend listened for a moment and said it was great. After days of this, he finally got the story: His pitch-perfect accent came with the simple grammar of a child. Everyone thought he was, as he put it, "touched in the head"!

In the same vein, one of my all-time favorite chapter headings is this one, from the 2015 reference book *Psycholinguistics: Introduction and Applications.* Lise Menn and Nina Dronkers open their chapter on the language disorder aphasia with "Why There's a High Cost to Being Slow and Sounding Weird: Who Do They Think I Am?"

I want to share some of the basics of grammar development as a way to show you that what children hear is processed and internalized long before they are capable conversationalists.

Origins of Grammar

There are fascinating lines of research into how grammar develops. At the big-picture level, there are still disagreements about whether grammar is innately wired into human brains or whether it is acquired based on statistical analysis. I tend toward the hybrid explanation. It seems clear that human capacity includes the propensity to learn grammar. That must come from somewhere. It is also the case that any human born on any part of the planet will learn whatever grammar or grammars they hear. So patterning and statistics must be at play also.

Using Grammatical Information to Determine Word Meaning

Children really are paying attention to what we say. Recall that morphemes are the smallest unit of speech that bears meaning. If you offer kids "a cookie" or "the cookie" or "some cookies," they know the difference. These small pieces of language are called *grammatical morphemes*.

The surprising thing is that even tiny bits of words like this can carry meaning. And young children learn this very early. Want to test it? Try this yourself: Put an *s* at the end of *cookie* and you'll have a very happy three-year-old! Kids also recognize that *a* versus *the* has meaning. Do you get one cookie? Or do you get the *last* one?

Young children are hearing and using this grammatical information to make sense of what we say to them. Pretty astonishing really.

Learning Verbs

Early research into language development focused on how children acquire the meaning of nouns. Naming objects for young children is a common practice across a multitude of languages, but it has also been shown that children learn and produce what their parents say, whether that is noun-intensive, verb-intensive, or a blend. Young children have also been found to produce the verbs that are more frequently used by their parents, and to use them in the same ways that their parents do.

In the introduction to their 2010 edited volume *Action Meets Word: How Children Learn Verbs*, Kathy Hirsh-Pasek and Roberta Golinkoff report on the current research into verb acquisition. The field is newly emerging, and there is much to be learned. Two findings are worth noting here though. In research across many languages, verbs have been found to be harder than nouns for young children to learn. This is because they refer to things that are less concrete, less apparent, and less permanent; because they are relational in their meaning; and also because they tend to have a wider range of possible definitions. Yet current cross-cultural research into verb acquisition also shows that the patterns of the native language influence the way in which children initially learn words.

Because language gives us power, children will learn the grammar of their native language(s) and will come to speak them correctly. There is more to using language, though, than just speaking grammatically correct sentences.

Pragmatics Research with Children

When we speak, our words, our tone, and our delivery all shape what others think we mean. This is effortless to show in my classes using just a couple of words because it is both auditory and visual. See if you can hear these in your head. Or better yet, try saying them out loud yourself:

"Nice dress." (smiling)
"Nice dress." (laughing playfully)
"Nice dress." (laughing nastily)
"Nice dress." (bored)

Our words, really, are not transparent. The tone, the attitude, the delivery—all these additional nuances pack meaning. Together they comprise the complete communication. Kids notice this very early on, and they respond in kind. Say something in a bubbly, excited, upbeat tone and watch how a kid responds to you. Say it in a flat or angry tone and watch the difference. When we speak to children, our words and tone both carry weight.

Kids are listening, and they imitate what they hear. Parents and teachers can expect to hear their own words coming out of a child's or teen's mouth. We all do this. So many parents are surprised, even mortified, to hear things their parents used to say to them coming out of *their own* mouths! There's nothing quite like realizing you sound like your mother.

My first instance of this was when my daughter turned two. Shortly before I was due to have our second child, friends gave our daughter a baby doll. She loved it and was very tender with it. The first time I saw her look upset with the doll, I was worried what I would hear next.

"We have to talk" coming out of a barely two-year-old's mouth is pretty funny. It gave me great pause though: I hadn't realized I said that! As I listened for it over the next few days, I was chagrined to hear it. *A lot.* No greater teacher than your child!

Another great reminder came a couple of years later, when our four-year-old daughter acted as interpreter for our two-year-old son—about me! She patiently explained to her brother, "When she says 'well . . . ,' she means 'no'." So matter of fact!

Speech Acts: Doing Things with Words

One of the main things that separates humans from other animals is language, specifically, our ability to use words to do things. This ability is called *speech acts*, and it is a powerful part of human language. All animals communicate. Even plants and trees communicate with one another, though we are only now starting to learn what those processes are. But to use your *words* to accomplish something—that's the power of speech.

Kids are drawn to language because of its power, and so they learn to respond and create their own speech acts. Children younger than two can use their words to get someone to stop bothering them. Children younger than three can use their words to help someone feel better. Children younger than four can use their words to work out a sharing agreement. It's heady, powerful stuff.

Given that children are so attuned to speech acts, it's worth asking what they're hearing. Is it mostly commands, like these?

> *"No."*
> *"Behave!"*
> *"Stop that!"*
> *"Sit down!"*
> *"Shut up!"*

Or is it something that will open their thinking more? In the rest of the book, I'll show how other ways of talking to kids can build their understanding, their memory, and their ability to control themselves.

Babies and preschoolers aren't just passive lumps, nor are they empty vessels waiting to be filled up. They are curious, active learners. That was one of the things my students reported at the end of the semester being the most surprised about.

Recent research offers insight into just how actively young children shape their language acquisition. Have you ever noticed that even if you can't hear the whole sentence someone says, you can often determine what they said? Humans are good at filling in the gaps of incomplete or ambiguous speech. It's a phenomenon well known to psychologists, and it's called the "noisy channel model." We take the sounds we actually hear (our perceptual input) and combine them with what we would expect, given the circumstances and what we know about the speaker (our expectations). What's fascinating is that young children—ages four and five—do this as well as adults do.

In a 2016 study that was both simple and clever, researchers led by Daniel Yurovsky, a psychologist at University of Chicago, showed adults and preschoolers pairs of photos accompanied by an audio description that was hard to make out. The goal was to figure out which of the two photos the speaker, "Katie," was describing. One photo showed a fairly conventional scene: for example, a cat with kittens. The other showed a less conventional scene—in this case, a cat with hammers. The speech was distorted so the listener had to infer what the speaker was more likely to be saying.

In the second phase of the study, the adults and preschoolers saw a new pair of photos accompanied by a new audio description. This time, the scenes depicted in the photos sounded almost identical, though again, one was more conventional and the other less so (e.g., a plate with carrots and *peas* or a plate with carrots and *bees*). In this round, the speaker always described the unconventional scene, but again, the sounds were muffled. How would listeners react? Would they simply choose what was more conventional as the likely target?

It turns out it depended on what was heard in phase 1. If "Katie" had described a plausible scene in round 1, a plausible scene was picked in round 2. However, if "Katie" had described an implausible scene the first time, that information was used to guide expectations of her in round 2. This was equally true for the forty-three preschoolers and the fifty adults who took part.

What this study tells us is that children are building models of what we are like. And they're using those models to guide what we hear from us, even if the background is noisy, or we mumble, or they just miss part of it because they're too absorbed in what they're doing. Even as young as age four, children can take incomplete or ambiguous perceptual input and combine it with what they know about us and the situation around us to make sense of incomplete speech. And the study showed that they do it just as easily and well as adults do.

What we say to kids shapes their thinking, in part through this kind of mechanism. They get to know us and they use what they learn to guide what we might be saying to them. Keep in mind that the study had very limited input from "Katie." A single instance was all it took to start forming expectations of what she might say in the future. But if we are interacting with children repeatedly over time, the dataset from which they draw is obviously much larger. Parents and teachers create an enormous amount of speech directed to children. All of it is going in and is being used to create their understanding of the world.

Words as Start Conditions

Words have a lot of power to influence thinking and work.

When my friend Nicole's son was a third grader, there was a funny moment at the parent-teacher-student conference. The teacher opened the conference by asking the student, "So, what are your strengths?" The young boy answered readily, "My legs. My legs are really strong. I can really kick a football."

The teacher's reaction to this unexpected answer was great. She listened, took in where he was, and built from what he gave her, replying, "You *are* strong. I've seen you on the field. And you're fast. What about your strengths in class?"

"Oh. Math." This nine-year old's notion of "strength" was clearly different from his teacher's!

How often do the words we hear trigger our thinking unconsciously?

I like the phrase *words as start conditions,* from Michael Dearing, a former lecturer at Stanford University's famed d.school. In a classroom activity he called "Factory vs. Studio," Dearing divided students into teams of four to work on a design challenge: produce a children's book for ages three to seven, with commercial appeal and merchandising potential. One team was set to work in the Factory and given the words *efficiency, production, industrial revolution,* and *division of labor.* The other team was set to work in the Creative Studio and given the words *joy! play! create!* and *fun!*

Dearing found that giving targeted starting points influenced his students' thinking and problem solving hugely. What's going on?

Each team's starting words drew on hidden associations the students had, leading the teams to very different styles of collaboration and very different end products. That's a classic example of *priming*, and it speaks volumes to how our words can influence what kids think.

Priming

Priming is a memory process that has to do with how we associate things. Any experience with something (it could be a person, object, or event) predisposes us to think more about it *and also* about other things that we relate to it. It readies us, in other words, to think about related ideas. We have activation networks running throughout our memories. They link ideas and experiences in ways that often aren't conscious.

Imagine I started asking you about the beach, for example. Just talking to you might bring up images of beaches and ping every memory you have of being at the beach or seeing beaches in movies and photos. You would be primed to think of obvious things like the ocean, waves, and sand. Maybe sunscreen and beach towels. But you would also be primed to think of less obvious things like seafood, sailing, every ocean creature you have ever heard of, and numerous other things your mind has connected to beaches.

This really does happen, and in a myriad of ways. For example, I spent a huge part of my childhood in Australia. Although it's an English-speaking country, it has a surprising amount of vocabulary that is unique. (Don't throw a wobbly! Right, mate? Ripper!)

I find any time I talk with Australians for even a brief time, all kinds of words I haven't used or thought of for ages come rushing to the surface. They're simply suddenly available in a way that they hadn't been moments before. In fact, the activation is so strong that it doesn't even have to be an Australian accent to trigger or prime my Aussie words. Pretty much anyone with a British-influenced accent will do!

The same thing happens for me with French, which I was near-fluent in at one point in my life. My French is activated any time I'm around people speaking a language other than English—even if it's not French! It's as if my brain goes "Not English? OK. French!" And I suddenly find myself thinking in French and primed to want a baguette.

Shaping Thought

I was introduced to the idea that what we say shapes what kids think through a different question: does the *particular* language we speak influence the ways in which we think?

This idea hit me first through anecdotes. I started graduate school in a developmental psychology department, as part of an international research group. Every single one of my colleagues from other countries talked about how they couldn't discuss their work in their native language. Having done all the thinking about their research in English, they found that they couldn't talk to people at home about what they were doing. I was particularly intrigued because each one felt it wasn't simply that they lacked the technical vocabulary in their home language (which was true). But really, they felt it was more than that—their entire conceptualization of what they were working on was in English, and they found they couldn't think about it in their other, *native*, language. That was astonishing to me, but it also made perfect sense.

Back when I was a graduate student, there were big academic disagreements about this question of whether language influences thought, called *linguistic relativity*. The ideas and work of linguistics pioneer Benjamin Whorf, previously discredited, were slowly being revisited and rethought. Whorfian thought was coming back, slowly, and being revised.

Over the years, many multilingual people have told me that they prefer one language to another for some form of their thinking. Most recently it was a former student who is trilingual. Justin mentioned that he uses the languages to his advantage, testing out ideas out in Japanese or Chinese to give himself a different perspective.

We now know some of the *cognitive* benefits of speaking more than one language—better working memory, for example. It's not a big stretch to imagine that other forms of thought are being shaped as well.

It wasn't long before I had a new question: if speaking different languages allows for different kinds of thinking, wouldn't that also be true for the different ways in which a *single* language is spoken?

Human beings are social creatures, born into communities of people who have ideas and values and norms, and a language for expressing those. In other words, we have a culture. And language is the primary vehicle for conveying that culture. It's not enough for a child to watch and learn. Language is an integral component of full understanding.

So when we think about language development in babies, kids, and teens, it begs the question: **why would we think it's the words only—and not also the underlying message?**

All words carry meaning beyond their surface use. "I'm fine" can mean so many things; "I love you," even more. How do we learn the words themselves *and* their intended meanings? How do we learn that the same word can have many nuanced meanings, sometimes even at the same time? How do we learn who gets to say which things? And how do we influence the world and other people through our language?

Entire fields of research are devoted to understanding this.

Psycholinguistics is the study of how we learn to use and understand language. Or perhaps it's better to say how we learn to produce language and to understand its use by other people.

An example of the impact of language from psycholinguistic research is that thinking about motion, whether real or abstract, influences our other thoughts in subtle and usually hidden ways. *Fictive motion* is the term for implied motion by things that can't actually move—trees running along the road, for example, or time stopping. When people hear fictive motion metaphors, it influences how they comprehend other things. Teenie Matlock, a former grad school colleague who now holds an endowed Chair at UC Merced, found that people draw different pictures for the description "trees run along the road" versus "trees running along the road." Running seems to imply a longer time period, and the drawings are longer—often extending into the distance. Hearing about real motion has a similar effect though. More recently, Matlock has also shown that when problem solving after reading stories about travel, people make faster judgments in the subsequent task if they have read about fast travel, shorter distances, or easy terrain. (If intrigued, see her chapter in the 2017 *Cambridge Handbook of Cognitive Linguistics*.)

Sociolinguistics is the study of language in its broader social and cultural contexts. It looks at how social categories and identities are constructed and maintained through language. That includes things like gender, race, and ethnicity, and also things like rank, prestige, and status.

An example of the impact of language from sociolinguistic research is that how you are introduced in a professional setting matters for how you are perceived. In high stakes settings, it can matter even more.

A 2017 study conducted at the prestigious Mayo Clinics found that male and female doctors introduced their colleagues differently for their important Grand Rounds presentations. Mayo physician Julia Files and colleagues found that Mayo's female doctors introduced virtually all their colleagues as *Dr.*, irrespective of the colleague's gender (96 percent of the time). Mayo's male doctors used *Dr.* only about two-thirds of the time; the other one-third, they used the colleague's first name. But not equally. Male doctors used the professional title *Dr.* for their *male* counterparts far more often (72 percent of the time versus only 49 percent for their female colleagues). More than half the time a male doctor introduced a female colleague, she was called by her first name. In a high stakes setting for career advancement, that kind of difference can play a subtle, unconscious role.

All of this is to offer you a clear perspective:

Children are listening to us.

Our words are going in.

Those words are shaping what and how children think.

Let's look at how we can use this to help kids grow into their best selves.

4

The Big Lessons

Who are we teaching them to be?

Our words are so powerful. They teach children who we are and who to become. In this chapter, we look at how language shapes the biggest lessons children learn from us. I discuss two key phrases you can use to guide your interactions with children. We'll look at three ideas trending in education today and how they speak to learning from our mistakes: growth mindset, compassion, and grit. The chapter closes with a look at how we communicate perhaps the most important lesson underpinning it all: that we hold the children in our lives with unconditional love *and* high standards.

Who Are We Teaching Our Children to Be?

In my undergraduate classes, I offered my students two phrases to guide every interaction they have with a child:

- Mistakes are opportunities to learn.
- What am I teaching in this moment?

I find these to be incredibly powerful reminders to be present with the child in front of me and to use this moment—each moment—to help them walk toward being the best person they can be. These phrases help us make better choices about what we say, knowing that our words are impacting children's *thinking* and the mindset they hold about the world.

"Mistakes are Opportunities to Learn"

Like most truisms, this phrase is at the same time both simplistic and profound. It's so easy to say that we want to learn from our mistakes. It's quite a different thing to act on that and live it every day. At the school my children attended, this phrase was repeated daily, everywhere. The teachers really lived by it and modeled it for their students. They guided them to walk through a situation when something went wrong, gently and lovingly, yet also with purpose. When mistakes were made, it was looked at as a good thing—sometimes even to be celebrated!

Then I noticed that I would hear my children say this, at the opening of any discussion we were having after they'd done something wrong. At first I thought they were just parroting something they'd heard in school. That's not uncommon. And honestly, at first that's all I thought it was. Slowly, I started to appreciate that they were internalizing it—that it meant more to them than just a slogan.

I could see that it was sinking in by how they conducted themselves in their conversations with me. My kids were not just quicker to own up to what they had done wrong, they were more comfortable doing so. They were more engaged in thinking about what would make the situation right again, or at least better. They were genuinely interested in seeking solutions.

I ultimately embraced this phrase and its philosophy *because* of how my kids were using it. I found it liberating. No need to hide from mistakes or to hide my mistakes from anyone else. It was so much better—personally and out in the world with the people who mattered to me—to be open about what I had done wrong/badly/unthinkingly/ineffectively. Acknowledge it not to get past it but to help myself look at it with curiosity for the ways in which it would help me grow. It was a very different perspective from the way I was brought up.

When we use the phrase, it shapes how we think about the world and how we act in it. I loved that my children were hearing this phrase and internalizing it for guidance in their own life. For the first time, I heard the idea that while we adults might be learning this attitude like a foreign language, the kids were growing up native in this language. It was obvious that it was easier for them to adopt it, to live it. I also saw that it was easy for my children to encourage and support others in seeing life this way. I began doing that as well.

The real turning point for me personally came through my university teaching. I needed to confront one of my undergraduate students, whom I had caught plagiarizing a paper. This happens about once a semester, and it's never a comfortable interaction. As usual, I lined up my evidence, scheduled a time to talk, and sat the student down to show what I had found and the conclusion I had drawn from it. She had submitted a paper that had borrowed heavily from someone else's work. Plagiarism is a form of cheating—you're using work that's already been created and passing it off as your own new idea in order to get credit. It has a heavy cost.

Mandy was very open when I confronted her. She said she had been dealing with a lot outside school. She told me she had freaked out and, as she put it, had "cut corners." She told me she was a very good student and had never done anything like this before (possible, but one does hear that a lot from students in these types of moments). She was distraught (again, very common). I looked at her and told her I had something to say that might sound corny, but that I truly believed. I told her that "mistakes are opportunities to learn."

She looked surprised. We talked briefly about what would happen next, as spelled out from day one in the course syllabus: Plagiarism results in a zero for the paper and the professor files an academic integrity report with the university (which is a big deal because if you get two of those, they throw you out of school). After reviewing these somewhat grim repercussions, I encouraged her to use this as the opportunity it *could* be for her. I reminded Mandy again that this incident and the resulting consequences did not mean she was failing the class. I assured her that I would not penalize her in any way after this. She left shaken.

So I was both delighted and a little surprised when Mandy appeared in the next class, ready to learn. I've seen students vanish after encounters like this—either too embarrassed to face me or too unwilling to face themselves. But Mandy showed up. She worked hard all semester. She didn't give up. She also didn't settle for being angry with me for the bad grade or the embarrassment of being called out for cheating. She wrote an outstanding term paper (turns out she really was a good student!). On the last day of the semester, after the final, Mandy gave me a huge hug and said *thank you*. She shared that she had taken what I said to heart, and used it, and she wanted to tell me how much it had meant to her.

Is it that Mandy believed the phrase? Or that I did? Either way, what we say to kids (and young adults) shapes their world.

"What Am I Teaching in This Moment?"

When adults work with children, they tend to assume a teaching stance. It's often unconscious, but this is something that shows up consistently in the research: adults tend to take any interaction with a child as an opportunity for teaching.

Given that predisposition, this prompt is amazingly helpful for anyone working with kids.

Kids can be fun, challenging, annoying, maddening, and confusing—sometimes all in the same instance. It's easy to lose sight of them as small people, and it's even easy to blow your stack at them. I've told my university students very openly that having your own children will take you to places of anger that you never thought you could go. They're a little shocked; apparently professors aren't supposed to say things like that.

The issue isn't *whether* or not you'll get frustrated, it's what you do about it. **Keeping a clear sight on two things really helps:**

1. Kids are just small people, with less experience and time on the planet.

2. They are learning from what you do, so it's good to ask, "What am I teaching in this moment?"

Keep in mind that's not "What do I *want* to be teaching?" It's "What am I *actually* teaching, given what I am saying and doing in this moment?"

When we stop to consider what our actions and words might be teaching, it slows us down and gives us the chance to be better people. Few among us actually want to teach children to erupt in frustration. Few among us want to teach children impatience. But that's what happens when we model it.

Asking ourselves what we're teaching in this moment allows us to see our words and actions through the eyes of the child in front of us. It allows us to try instead to teach what is of value and to do that in a more respectful, loving way. That in itself is a huge lesson for children to absorb.

So in any moment, whether a quiet moment or a moment of acceptance, playfulness, or frustration, it's good to ask yourself, **What am I teaching in this moment?** *Because that will show you what the child is learning about . . .*

- Him/herself
- Me as a parent/teacher/adult
- What our family/school/group values are
- Life

These are profound questions. When we talk to children, we are conveying so much more than just the words we use. We are conveying our values. And it speaks directly to children and teens. They read our voices and our messages, and they take away lessons about who they are and what matters. Over time, these messages become ingrained. These messages lead to who the child becomes.

Who are we teaching them to be?

It's easy to lose sight of this in the heat of an argument or as you're running late out the door. It's easy to forget this as you're corralling a rowdy group of kids in an after-school program, or in a classroom, or an athletic field. It's easy to lose sight of, but it's worth training ourselves to remember what we are teaching.

When we yell at kids for screwing up, or ask things like "What were you thinking?!" we teach them that they deserve to be yelled at. We teach them that we are a person who yells and is intolerant. And that that is acceptable in our family or classroom. We teach them that when they do things wrong, it is shameful.

When we are accepting of kids, even when they make mistakes, and ask things like, "Wow—that didn't work out well; what should we do now?" we teach them that they are not defined by their mistakes. We teach them that we love them and also want them to do their best. And that in our classroom or family we help each other. We teach them that mistakes are opportunities to grow.

The language we use with children translates to their self-concept and then their concept of the world. This is critical to understand: the words we use are a huge part of their cognitive development and the mindset they take with them through life.

Things to Try

1. The next time a child does something that makes you crazy, stop and remind yourself that your next move will be teaching them something. What is it you want them to learn from this?

2. At a quiet time, reflect on what is important for you to convey to the children in your life about who they are. Start to ask yourself how you can create more of that in your interactions with them.

3. Remembering that we're teaching life lessons at every moment is hard to do. It's helpful to plan in advance to have a way to jog your memory. Maybe it's looking into the child's eyes or saying the word *teaching* to yourself. What kind of prompt would help you recall it at important moments?

Learning from Mistakes

The idea that we can learn from our mistakes is not new, or news. It permeates many places, cultures, and religions. Walking it is a different story, though. What is it that helps kids build their capacity to use their mistakes to move them forward? The story about my former student Mandy points to ideas that are trending today: growth mindset, compassion, and grit.

Growth Mindset

In her book *Mindset: The New Psychology of Success,* Carol Dweck distinguishes between two different approaches to life: a growth mindset that sees intelligence as something permeable and to be developed and a fixed mindset that sees intelligence as something that is unchanging and innate. Her extensive research shows that people with a fixed mindset fear taking risks, tend to avoid situations that are challenging, and resent the successes of others. That doesn't describe a very happy person.

Dweck talks about how she herself grew up with a fixed mindset. Through her research, she learned to see another way and worked hard to retrain herself to take the more flexible approach. It can be learned. But like the kids at my children's elementary school, growing up natively in that kind of language and environment makes it *much* easier!

Embracing the idea that mistakes are opportunities to learn doesn't mean coasting through life screwing up and moving on. It means actually taking responsibility for understanding and growing from our lapses. When kids are brought into this approach, they can learn it quite easily. That said, people do vary in their level of risk aversion. Welcoming mistakes may be counter to a child's temperament, but with consistent support, it can indeed become their default way of operating.

What was it that enabled Mandy to hear—and make use of—my offer? It's impossible to know exactly. But I think the way I teach is highly consistent with the philosophy about mistakes and also highly consistent with what Dweck calls the growth mindset. When you model this over time, it influences what people believe and how they behave.

Compassion

I find that compassion also fits well with the idea that mistakes are opportunities to learn. The growing buzz about compassion has brought a flood of new research, and the term is moving rapidly into the mainstream. Compassion can be defined as the feeling of tenderness or concern that arises when we see someone else suffering and it leads us to be motivated to help. It can also be extended to one's self. Once disparaged as soft or ineffectual, compassion is being shown to promote everything from happiness to the corporate bottom line.

In her 2016 book *The Happiness Track*, Emma Seppälä presents cutting edge research into the benefits of compassion. Seppälä is in a good position to know: she is simultaneously at Stanford University as Science Director for the Center for Compassion and Altruism Research (CCARE) and at Yale University as codirector of a project at the Center for Emotional Intelligence. Her chapter "Understand the Kindness Edge: Why Compassion Serves You Better Than Self-Interest" addresses the impact of compassion not only on relationships and health, but also on business, status, and employee loyalty. Tellingly, she says that "self-focus makes you weak in the face of failure" (2016, 146).

In order to take fully the opportunity that a mistake offers, the adult must hold the child compassionately in how he or she talks. It's hard for a child (or anyone) to make a mistake and be called on it.

Remember what we've seen throughout this book: What we say to children shapes what they think and how they feel. In helping a child use a mistake as a learning opportunity, we need to talk kids through the whole thing: identifying the mistake, talking about how it happened, figuring out what can be done to rectify it, and also explicitly how to learn from it. This is best done candidly. Yet it also needs the lightness that compassion brings. Our words, our tone, and the message we convey will make or break the child's ability to grasp the opportunity to learn.

Children must hold themselves compassionately as well. This may be an alien concept for most of us. Recall that fixed mindsets lead a person to avoid failure. Failure doesn't feel good to them. And as a result, kids who approach life this way will work to avoid the sense of failure that a mistake reveals. Having self-compassion allows for facing difficult emotions and situations, and being able to learn from them.

It can take a lot of support at times to help a child through this discomfort. That kind of support requires being sensitive to the child's feelings, while also encouraging them to stay open to looking at the mistake. It's quite an art.

I saw this firsthand when my son was in first grade. He had been at a different school for kindergarten. His teacher had been wonderful, but there had been a lot of bullying in the play yard; my young son had closed down by the end of the year. It was heartbreaking to see, and I was hoping that the move to the new school would help him regain his sense of joy and self-comfort.

Early in the school year, we had a near calamity. At the urging of a classmate, my son threw a rock up into the air in a crowded playground. It came down on another child. The boy's head got cut; mercifully, he was not gravely injured. In some schools, this could have resulted in suspension or expulsion. In my children's school, this was seen as a very important learning opportunity.

My tenderhearted son was horrified that he had hurt someone. So horrified, in fact, that he found it easier to blame someone else. The teacher worked closely with my son, helping him see where he had had choices and how he was responsible for his own actions. It resulted in him asking to go visit the boy who was hurt and choosing one of his own beloved stuffed animals to take to his classmate so that he would feel better. They worked it out while playing and had a great year together.

It's hard when your child is injured not to hold enmity toward whoever caused it. I was grateful to the boy's mother, both for allowing my son's efforts to make amends and for seeing him for who he truly was: a kind little boy who had made an awful mistake.

Was that one mistake all it took? Hardly. He learned some and kept growing. He had entered first grade already quite unwilling to risk much of himself. His teacher tackled it head on. When he made mistakes, she celebrated them—right down to cheering! She helped him first consider the possibility that he could learn from them and ultimately to be open to initiating that process. It was a long but successful year.

Similarly, I think compassion—both mine for her and her own for herself —was part of what enabled my student Mandy to return to class, work hard, and *thank me* at the end of the semester.

Grit

Another term that's getting a lot of press these days is *grit*. In her seminal book, *Grit: The Power of Passion and Perseverance*, Angela Duckworth says grit isn't simply hard work, but hard work on something you love to the point of expertise or achievement.

In terms of this book and the idea that what we say to kids shapes how they think and feel, I find *Grit* with a capital G highly problematic. That hard work can lead us to achieve well is not arguable. The question is: what are we saying about it, and what are kids hearing and coming to believe?

Duckworth's work has been widely taken up, and probably misrepresented in the process. Duckworth herself has been reported as saying it's been misconstrued (as has Dweck about her growth mindset work). When big ideas are oversimplified, the result can be very misleading. But I have some very big misgivings about capital-G grit.

My biggest concern about grit is that it's about the success more than the hard work. Duckworth's version of grit is about what it takes to attain extraordinary accomplishment. I worry about the messages that get sent to kids in the guise of hard work.

For one thing, grit as a life philosophy overlooks a lot of real social inequity. Not everyone who works that hard is going to achieve great success. Furthermore, it is a stark truth that not everyone has access to the opportunities that make that kind of effort possible. (And, in counterpoint, not all success is the result of that level of devotion; money, luck, and looks have a lot to do with who attains extraordinary success in life.) The danger is that if grit is lauded as the pathway to achievement, kids can be (and *are*) told that their failure to achieve is due to their own lack of effort or "grittiness."

For another, I worry even more about what the adoration of grit says about what's valuable in life. What do we mean by *success*? Do we allow for and instill in kids a belief that life success is more than what's equated with extraordinary levels of achievement?

Take, for example, Duckworth's lavish praise for student David Luong, who studied "hours and hours. Not in a week, but in a single day." Duckworth details his rise through her class— his move to an accelerated track; double-major in college; and PhD from UCLA. Luong is clearly an academic success story.

But 1) How do we know there weren't other students working just as hard? (Or is the proof supposed to be that they didn't make it like he did?)

And 2) Do all versions of success really come down to this kind of hard work?

When we laud grit, what exactly are we promoting?

I realize Duckworth acknowledges that grit is not the only or even the single most important thing to cultivate: "greatness and goodness are different, and if forced to choose, I'd put goodness first" (2016, 273). Placed a mere five pages from the end of the book, though, this comes as a bit of a throw-away thought. Is it really an either/or? Can't excellence and achievement arise *within* the context of doing and being good?

Note, too, that Duckworth herself says that *other qualities are better tied to learning* (2016, 274). She identifies three "virtue clusters" of character, and links them to the life outcomes they predict:

• *Intrapersonal* virtue includes grit and self-discipline, which Duckworth says her research shows predicts academic achievement (think grades and test scores).

• *Interpersonal* virtue includes the characteristics that make us "deeply good" and predicts positive social functioning and extent of friend networks.

• *Intellectual* virtue includes characteristics that "encourage active and open engagement with the world of ideas," such as curiosity and zest, which Duckworth says predicts "a positive, independent posture toward learning."

Tell me. Which one is going to matter in life success defined more broadly? Test scores and grades? Or a positive outlook on learning?

If we want kids to be willing and able to learn from their mistakes, what qualities should we be cultivating in them? Curiosity and a growth mindset lead. Compassion too will help them. Grit—not so much. Duckworth may hold that it does, but I've seen too many people who become wedded to their notion of excellence, of the pursuit of it, who don't question what they're doing; they simply buckle down and push harder. In a 2017 article posted on the *Psychology Today* blog, happiness researcher Emma Seppälä tackled this very problem. In criticizing grit, Seppälä separated the idea of pursuing your goals no matter what, from pursuing them in a way that is sustainable and marked by self-care.

Perseverance and passion *can* lead human beings to extraordinary things. Learning to temper that so that our mistakes can be embraced and used to move us forward takes more, though. Our beliefs come across in the language we use and the messages we send to the children in our lives—in our homes and in our classrooms. How we speak to kids will shape whether they embrace the chance to learn from their mistakes.

Things to Try

1. Start by thinking rather than talking. Try to remember a time that you made a mistake you feel bad about. What have you learned from it? Now consider this: how would it change how you act in the future if you let go of feeling bad and just appreciated what you have learned to do differently?

2. The next time you're with a child who makes a mistake, try to catch yourself before you get upset/frustrated/angry. See if you can introduce the idea that "mistakes are opportunities to learn" and help the child find a useful lesson in what went wrong.

3. The next time you make a mistake in the presence of children, do this for yourself out loud so they can hear you walk through the process. Seeing you face your own mistakes will help them understand how to do it for themselves.

What Are We Telling Them?

My giant undergraduate class on child development included a service learning component. During the semester, students had to work twenty hours at a local community organization serving infants, children, or youth to help them see the course ideas in action. Most of our partner programs served very low-income kids who were facing the kinds of multiple risk factors that can pile up on families dealing with poverty.

At the start of the semester, we had a presentation day when representatives from the various partner organizations gave a short talk on their organization and what students would be doing with them. The reps were very upfront with my students: the kids they would be helping might not have an adult in their home life who was sober or committed to them. My students could have a unique and powerful impact.

After the panel presentations, I would stress to my students, every semester, that the developmental science is clear on this point: what kids need in their life is at least one person who holds high expectations for them AND who loves them unconditionally. And that the crazy thing was, they might be *that* person for a child they were going to meet and work with this semester. As trite as that sounds, I let them know it was a real thing.

You could always read the disbelief in their faces across the auditorium. And yet, without fail, in their end-of-semester reflection papers, several of them would come back and say something along the lines of, "You know, I thought you were over the top with that thing at the beginning, but this kid I'm working with has really opened up to me." The ones I really loved reading extended that commitment with declarations like,

"I know my twenty hours are over, but I can't stop now. I'm going to work at my service learning site through the rest of the year."

Unconditional love *and* very high standards.

Kids of all ages and backgrounds need this kind of support. We must show them that we have high expectations of them. And at the same time, these kind of high expectations must be tempered with an unconditional love—not the Tiger Mom kind of rigid standards, but the loving-them-into-a-better-place kind of standards: *You can do this. You can do better. I'm not going to let you screw this up. I'm here to help.*

Teen expert Josh Shipp puts it this way in a story about his own childhood. A former foster child, Shipp hit a life-changing point when he was fourteen. After stealing and crashing a car, he expected to be thrown out of his new foster home. It was what he was trying for, in the way that demoralized people often seek to undermine any chance of success or happiness. His new foster parent Rodney gave him an unexpected perspective: "We don't see you as a problem, son—we see you as an opportunity."

That language shook Shipp out of his self-destructive bent and set him on a path that would lead him to a job and eventually a career helping teens and their parents. In talks and on his website, Shipp says that the lesson he took away from that experience was this: "Every kid is ONE caring adult away from being a success story." As the science and many people attest, that's all it takes: just one caring adult and a life can be changed.

Unconditional love and very high standards held simultaneously are communicated through what we say. They shape what kids believe about themselves and their life— whether they have hope, or faith, that something better lies ahead.

How we talk to kids communicates the standards we hold for them and our opinion of them. The goal is leading them to understand, through our words, without always needing to say it directly:

I love you.

I respect you.

You matter.

What you do matters.

When kids grow up knowing this to their core, it shapes them to be strong, confident adults who have more to give to others.

Things to Try

1. Apart from the obvious, consider what you can say to the children in your life to tell them you love them no matter what.

2. What does unconditional love mean to you? How do you want to be expressing it?

3. Straddling the line between high expectations and warmth can be tricky for some of us. What messages of high standards did you grow up with? Are they helpful to you?

5

Shifting the Language of Control

Say what you *do* want

"No." Kids hear it all the time, and it often means nothing. I'd like to suggest that *no* is actually not all that helpful. A couple of words in my own defense first:

1. This isn't about giving kids everything they want—far from it. (Besides, many parents I hear issuing no's turn them to yes after enough pestering.)
2. This isn't about *never* saying no. A well-placed, authoritative "No!" can be a great safety tool. It can even stop a kid in their tracks if they're unaccustomed to hearing it.

This chapter is about seeing how what we say is understood by kids, and how that shapes their behavior now and in the future. "No" leads them to think, "OK, not this, but what?" There are much more effective ways to get at what we want from kids than just telling them no.

What If It's Not About Controlling Kids?

Let's start with this: why do we say no in the first place? Life happens and we bark out things like "No!" "Quit it!" "Stop that!" or "Don't do that!" Kids, especially young kids, do things we don't want them to. All the time. Your Facebook feed might be full of these things. It's the stuff that makes emoticons worth using!

"My daughter took the knobs off her dresser. After drawing on it!"
"My son climbed out of his crib during nap time ... "

If you aren't getting stories like this from friends and family, just go to YouTube. Ever heard of the peanut butter kid? If not, go Google it. It's still one of the funniest things I've ever seen.

And yet, we can't watch young children 24/7. That's called helicopter parenting, and there's plenty of information out there about how unhelpful it is.

So how do we control them? How do we make kids do what we want?

The short answer is: We don't.

Obviously we can't let kids run amok, but I'm questioning the overarching goal: control. I'm arguing that the goal of parenting, and of good teaching, is to help children develop their own ability to control themselves.

And in case you're thinking, "Oh, so I should just throw my hands up and let them do whatever they want? You're crazy!" I'm talking about something *much harder*.

When was the last time you learned how to do something new? Was it easy? Didn't you screw up a lot at the beginning? Did it get easier? This is what I'm talking about. **Learning is messy. It takes time.** Yet I find it's often hard for adults in the US to find the middle ground between *overcontrol* and *no control*.

No control is a disaster. A friend told me this story about his friend Kelly. She decided when her first child was born never to say no to him—she didn't want to stifle him. What's worse, her child could say no to her, but she couldn't say no to him!

As you might guess, it didn't work out well.

This mom bent over backwards to accommodate her child. It exhausted her and put a strain on her friendships. Out shopping one day, her little boy wanted to play with the steering wheel in the parking lot. Kelly didn't want to say no, so she tried to convince him to go inside. But he didn't want to. So they sat there. For an hour and a half! Until he was ready. (And yes, these days, she says no to her second son. And to her first son as well!)

But overcontrol is unhelpful too. Kids need room to explore and develop their own interests, to screw up and learn from those mistakes. And control itself is a mixed bag.

For example, I saw this promotional offer online: "No means no: how to teach your child that you mean business." Frankly, if you need to teach them that, I think you're already up the creek without a paddle.

What this book should help you see is that the way you talk to kids shapes what they think and understand. If you have to tell them you're in control, well, you're not. It's like the advertising world. When they have to put *delicious* on the packaging, you can be pretty sure it won't be.

So how do we walk a middle line? It's hard for kids to appropriately control themselves. *And* that looks different as kids age—so for a young child, a school-aged child, or a teen, it's going to be a different, and moving, target.

In her Positive Discipline program, Jane Nelson calls this "kind *and* firm." It's an idea I find my students have a hard time with. How is it possible to be both of these at the same time?

What if I show you it's possible to steer kids away from what you *don't* want and toward what you *do* want, without having to control them all the time? What if I show you that by doing that, you even help kids build their self-regulation skills? It starts by understanding what kids hear when they hear "No."

Compliance or Resistance

Children hear the word "No" a lot. When quirky pop band They Might Be Giants released their first album of children's songs in 2002, it was simply called *No!* The title song is a hilarious take on the totality of no in kids' lives. The problem is that when we say no to a child, we offer them only one of two possible avenues: compliance or resistance.

Most children, especially young children, actually do *want* to do the right thing. They will stop what they're doing maybe out of fear of reprisal, but also out of wanting to please you. The problem is: they can't *stay* stopped.

So having complied, briefly, they are usually drawn right back to the same activity. It's interesting to them. Something about it feels good or intrigues them, or they're bored and haven't thought of anything else to try.

So they go back to it. And they get another "Quit it!" or "Stop that!" or "I told you to stop that!" So now you're on the merry-go-round. And not the fun kind.

On top of that, in order to comply, you have to actually understand what's being asked of you. So, for example, "Quit it!" only works if a child genuinely understands what they're doing that you don't like. It may seem hard to believe, but often young children have no idea what aspect of what they're doing you want them to stop. It may seem painfully obvious to you, but they're coming at it from a completely different point of view. They may not know what the problem is.

And again, if they do stop, it's hard to stay stopped. So even if you get it, compliance isn't a permanent thing.

Years ago, when my son was in the terrible twos, a friend loaned me her *Love and Logic* tapes. I didn't agree with everything authors Jim Fay and Foster Cline had to say, but I certainly found them a breath of fresh air compared to the overly conscientious, politically correct view. Two pieces stuck with me:

1. Slot machines and consistency

The point is that anyone working with children needs to be consistent. Every time. If you're not, just like a gambler at a slot machine who keeps playing because there is a *possibility* of a big win, kids will keep taking shots to see if you'll give in this time.

My analogy is those velociraptors in the first *Jurassic Park* movie, testing the fence: "Is it still on?... Zap! Is it still on?... Zap! Is it still on?... Ooh. I got through!" (And, yes, now we're *all* in trouble!)

2. A story about bedtime

One of the authors' young sons loved to get out of bed and come find his parents in the night. Sweet, maybe. Endearing, possibly. But also a real deal-breaker for a solid night's sleep and being able to maintain any kind of equilibrium as a parent.

So the story had me in stitches—he didn't tell the boy no at all. In fact, he welcomed him into their bed. He let his son get settled in, comfy, cozy, and pretty happy with himself. And then slowly, he proceeded to roll on to him so that he was squished and uncomfortable! Guess who decided he didn't want to stay after all?

It's one of the funniest stories I've ever heard from a parent. It also reminded me that "no" not only isn't always necessary, there may in fact be other, much more effective routes.

Flipping Our Negative Commands

An exercise I did with my senior-level cognitive development students works very well to demonstrate this idea of 'not saying no.' Think of anything you might tell a child to stop: *No running! Quit that! Don't push her!* Now take a moment to **reword that same command**, phrased in terms of **what you actually want the child to be doing.**

I call this using negative commands versus saying what you *do want*. Some examples are: "Eyes only!" versus "Don't touch!" and "Walking feet!" versus "No running!" After many years of working in elementary classrooms, I find this one helpful: "You need a tissue" versus "Don't pick your nose!"

I had my undergrads break into pairs to do this with a partner and come up with at least three examples of a command they'd used or heard before, along with a more positive way of wording it. It's easier to do together—and more fun—but try it now, wherever you are.

Students would come back with all sorts of ideas. For some of my students, this exercise was so easy it was almost confusing as to why we were doing it. For others, it was so alien, they could only come up with one or two examples. Seeing that range amongst their classmates was always a valuable discussion point for my students.

Here are a few ideas routinely suggested by my students, many of whom support themselves by working as nannies, preschool aides, coaches, or waitstaff:

- "Inside voices" versus "No yelling!"
- "Gentle touches" versus "No hitting!"
- "Hands to yourself" versus "Don't touch them!"

I wanted my students to see that you can flip any negative command into something that more clearly directs the child to the desired behavior. But this isn't just about how kids behave. This is fundamentally about their cognitive development.

What we say shapes what kids think.

Helping children conceptualize what is wanted from them helps them regulate their own actions and also helps them remember how to do so in the future. This is especially true for young children, who need considerable support from the adults in their lives. But it's just as applicable for school age kids and teens.

What's Going On In Kids' Heads?

Specifically, saying what you *do* want activates three distinct aspects of cognition:

- Self-regulation
- Elaboration
- Internalization

Why does it work this way? It's worth a quick dip into child development theory. There are many competing theories, each of which is useful for understanding different aspects of kids' lives. All theories exist to explain what we've seen and help us predict what's ahead. Explaining kids is more complicated than you might imagine!

In terms of children's *cognitive* development there are three main theories: Jean Piaget's theory of constructing knowledge, Lev Vygotsky's theory of social action, and Information Processing theories of memory and thinking. Each offers important perspective on why saying what you do want develops these three aspects of kids' thinking:

1. Self-regulation

The two principal theories of child development are from Piaget and Vygotsky. Both yield deep insights into child self-regulation.

Piaget and Self-regulation

From a Piagetian perspective, you can think of children as developing from the inside out. Piaget theorized that all human thinking develops as we interact with the world and bump up against something new: we either *assimilate* the new information and fit it into what we already know, or we have to *accommodate* our understanding to make room for this new bit. This ongoing process of *adaptation* takes us to new and deeper levels of development from birth to death.

If you've held a newborn baby, you know that children come into the world unable to regulate or direct any of their motions. Over the first eighteen months of life, they quickly start to flex their muscles and learn to move their bodies in ways that are coordinated and deliberate. They do this by building on nothing more than the reflexes all humans are born with. Babies first marshal their own bodies, then become able to incorporate movement with objects, then to combine multiple actions, and then to experiment with how objects in the world behave under different circumstances. All in less than two years.

By the age of two, Piaget found, children move beyond merely responding to the world and begin to represent it in new mental ways. From age two to about age seven, they are working on increasing their ability to make and hold mental images, and also on understanding that the world can be understood using categories. From seven to roughly eleven or twelve, those categories become things they can reason about and compare, and the complexity of the world becomes something they can work with more easily.

At the last stage of development, Piaget found that from about age twelve onward, children and adults can work with multiple categories at a time, in systematic ways, and that those categories can be layered together in nets of relationships. Along the way, children move from understanding the world at a surface level—what is literally available to them to perceive—to a deeper, more internal level.

What's that have to do with self-regulation? From a self-regulatory perspective, Piaget shows us that children will regulate their bodies before their ideas, and they will regulate themselves in a surface way before an interior one. Another way to put this: they can stop their hands and feet and motion before they can marshal the ideas driving their behavior. And they can regulate the obvious, visible things before they can control their emotions and thoughts.

To help them exert that self-control, you can see that it would help not just to give them the information about what we want them to stop, but also to give them the information about what we want in its place. This allows them to direct their attention to regulating their bodies in ways that comply with the new command.

Vygotsky and Self-regulation

From a Vygotskian perspective, you can think of children as developing from the outside in. Vygotsky comes at all of this from a very different perspective. He theorized that all human thinking develops first within the context of doing things with others (within social activity), and that our thinking moves from something we do with others to gradually being able to do on our own (internally). This process of *internalization* moves us forward in our development from birth to death.

Children come into the world unversed in the ideas, behaviors, language, or customs of their communities. They learn these through interaction with those communities. Vygotsky argued that in all we do, we learn first with or from others.

Babies demonstrate this in their need for human interaction, in their innate preference for human speech from human faces, and in their ability to copy us. For babies, that need is paramount. They are unable even to move themselves for months. It takes a few years to master the language and many more years before they are thinking with the complexity of an adult. And that's fine. Much of what we do as people we don't need to be completely independent for.

What's that have to do with self-regulation? From a self-regulatory perspective, Vygotsky shows us that children will be regulated first by others and then gradually by their own efforts. They will need support from the people and objects in their world as they move more and more into mastery.

To help them exert that self-control, you can see that saying what you *do* want gives kids the tools directly.

2. Elaboration

Elaboration is an idea taken from Information Processing, a field that draws the analogy of human thinking to computers, in that human thinking also "processes" information. Elaboration is a key process for remembering and, ultimately then, for learning. It is hooking new information onto existing knowledge structures so that the new information can be more readily retained and retrieved. When we elaborate, in the Information Processing sense of the word, we use what we already understand to make sense of the new information. By anchoring it to something that's already understood, we stand a better chance of remembering it when we need it the next time.

Saying what we want children to do, rather than use a simpler negative command, gives children elaborative power. When we say, "We need to wait our turn" or "Eyes only," we cue children to things they already understand and help them conceptualize what it is we want from them.

3. Internalization

Internalization brings us back to Vygotsky. To truly learn something, one must be able to think it on their own. That's the difference between skill acquisition and mastery.

Saying what you do want versus using a negative command works better because it gives children (and especially young children) the tools they need to deeply internalize what is expected of them.

Think Legos as an example. It's far more potent and long-lasting to help a preschooler recognize that "this shelf is for other people's Lego projects and you can only look at them," than to simply tell that child not to touch. Saying "don't touch" doesn't help for long, it doesn't sink in as far, and it doesn't help children control themselves better in the future.

When we internalize, or master, something, it is ours to use again and again. We can draw on it any time we wish. Wouldn't you rather have children who could do that without needing the constant reminders, the frustrated "No!"s, and the "Didn't I tell you not to do that?!"

Things to Try

1. Listen for the next time you tell a child "No." Start by trying to rephrase what you're saying to avoid the no.

2. Taking self-regulation as the goal, rephrase what you want from the child to give them the exact words to follow.

3. Thinking in terms of elaboration, what can you say that this child already understands to help them do what it is you want?

Saying What We *Do* Want—Instead of What We Don't

Saying what we *do* want gives kids all these tools to build from: self-regulation, elaboration, and internalization. It becomes part of their skillset.

There is also compelling evidence from the field of psycholinguistics that saying what we *don't* want just doesn't work very well. It comes from the area called *negation processing.*

Have you ever been at a pool where the lifeguard was blowing the whistle and yelling, "No running!"—and the kid just kept going? Partly, it's because kids are oblivious when they're playing. But partly, it's also because **when we hear a negative command, what we process is the positive version.** In other words, what that kid speeding along the pool deck is hearing in their head is "Running!" It's way more effective when the lifeguard blasts the whistle and yells, "Walk!"

Negation processing happens when we encounter a negative version of an idea. A common example in negation research literature is "The bird is in the air" versus "The bird is not in the air." If you were asked to match a picture to each of these sentences, you might choose a flying bird for the first sentence and a bird on the ground or in a nest for the second one. "The bird is not in the air" is a bit awkward, but we get what it means.

A 2016 edited volume examined the state of the art on experimental work in negation. As summarized by Ye Tian and Richard Brehany, researchers in negation processing largely agree on two main findings:

1. Negative sentences are harder for people to process. They take longer to read, are more prone to errors, and are harder to remember.

2. In many cases, when people hear a negative sentence, their initial response is to represent the *positive* version in their head. In other words, hearing "The bird is not in the air," we initially process it as if what was said was "The bird is in the air" and we initially picture a *flying* bird in the sky.

Language processing happens on an unconscious level and instantaneous timescale. To capture it, the research on this is conducted in milliseconds, using what's referred to as an interstimulus interval (ISI) to measure a person's reaction to the input.

A millisecond is very short. It's one-thousandth of a second. So 250 milliseconds is just one-quarter of a second.

In negation processing research, it is robustly found that in the 250-millisecond ISI range, after hearing a negative sentence, it is the *positive* form of a sentence that is being represented. There's also strong evidence to suggest that this continues up until about a 1500-millisecond ISI. Only after that point—in other words, one-and-a-half seconds after the input—is the negative form correctly represented and available to guide a person's actions.

One of the key researchers in this field is Barbara Kaup, of Tübingen University in Germany. Her work examines the relationship between the ideas we hold in our working memory and our comprehension of language. As Kaup has found, when people are asked to match the sentence "Sam forgot to wear his hat" or "Sam did not forget to wear his hat" to a stick figure drawing of a man with or without a hat on his head, it takes longer to match the second, negative sentence than to match the first. People are also more likely to make mistakes doing this and are more prone to misremembering the sentence.

Think about processing time. For the first one to one-and-a-half seconds following a negated statement, we will be thinking of the positive form of it. Now think about how impulsive children are. They process quickly and keep moving. If their reaction time is under one-and-a-half seconds—and it often is—they will be working off the positive version of the sentence. That's the "Running!" version instead of "No running!" for that kid by the pool.

My teenage daughter told me recently that she uses this idea all the time at work. She works for a children's theatre company, wrangling up to thirty-five young children backstage. (Not my idea of fun, but she loves it!) She said she's used this approach since I first told her about it ten years ago. So, for example she'll say, "Keep your feet off the chairs and on the floor please," telling the kids exactly what she does want from them.

I'm certainly not alone in seeing the importance of this. I was delighted when I received a recent newsletter from an educator I follow. Sexual health educator Anya Manes helps parents become better able to speak with their kids about topics that are hard to discuss (more on this in Chapter 12, "The Hard Stuff," in the section "Being Open About Difficult Things"). In her newsletter, she urged parents to "teach what *to* do, rather than what *not* to do." Manes argued that our warnings against risks like getting pregnant or sexual assault are less effective than teaching kids how to know and talk about their own boundaries.

We can see then that saying what you *do* want rather than what you *don't* want is very powerful.

How does it work?

Here's what it looks like in action: A preschooler (age three or four) is playing and a baby comes over. The preschooler knows that they should share, but the baby starts pawing through the toys, and a little hand shoots out to grab a toy away from the baby. Baby keeps exploring, and soon the preschooler is "playfully" pushing the baby away.

What do you say?

A lot of parents will get loud at this point: "No, Jana!" Some will use the typical classroom phrases *No, thank you*, or *please stop*. But this situation needs more—more words and possibly even more actions.

Playing with a little four-year-old recently, I saw him struggling to overcome his desire to keep the toys to himself, away from his baby brother. His baby brother had recently started standing, newly able to explore more actively. The family lives in a very small, one-room space, so it's not possible for this little boy to play separately. As the baby came for the toys, again and again, the older boy started messing with the baby, squishing his cheeks, being rough with him. Their mom tried the old standards—"No, Javier!" and "Please, no!" increasingly louder. She was concerned about the baby's well-being, and she wanted her older son to be good with him. She just didn't have a big set of tools for supporting that growth.

Javier had turned four very recently, so I played to his ego. I started by reminding him that he was bigger, that the baby was smaller, and that he needed to be gentle with him. I redirected his play to the toys he had. I reiterated that it would be OK if the baby played with some of the toys.

We went through this two or three times, and I could see he wasn't lessening his roughness, so I bumped it up. I showed Javier his arms and his muscles, saying that he had gotten big and strong but that the baby was still very little. He wasn't strong yet like Javier, so Javier needed to be gentle with him. It would be OK if the baby played with a few of the toys. We did this same thing a couple of times, and slowly I watched Javier relax into having his brother play next to us. The pushing stopped, and he fell to being fully engaged with the toys.

Was it my words solely? I'd be a fool to say it was. It was a combination of so many things—my words, my actions, my tone of voice, my proximity, and also my attention to and on him. And this approach has to be repeated—many, many times. However, hearing the *what* (be gentle), the *why* (he's smaller), and *how to proceed* (let him play) gives Javier the mental tools he needs to restructure his behavior. It won't transform in one day, of course. When I see him again next week, I'm going to try it again. Slowly, the idea that being stronger and bigger means needing to care for his brother will sink in. And he will be able to use those words in his head to help him not push on the baby.

Here's another example: "Use the towel, not your pants." How many of us have heard ourselves say something like this? Use the napkin, not your clothes; use a tissue, not your sleeve . . . It's a common theme. Heck, it's reportedly why army uniforms initially had decorative buttons on the outside of the sleeve!

Painting with four-year-old Javier in his family's room, I brought a mat to put underneath everything and a towel for cleanup. A couple of preschool projects lying around showed he had access to painting at school, but I hadn't seen any paints at home. Like most little boys, Javier loves to explore the materials (read: "make a mess"). He wasn't as interested in the watercolor paints themselves, as in how they turned the water different colors.

Javier and I started to work with the watercolors, and almost immediately he wiped his brush across his pants. I showed him the towel: "Here's a towel I brought with me, so you can wipe your hands on it and not get paint on your clothes." This was repeated in some form probably four or five more times—always mixing it up a little so I didn't sound like a broken record! And always offering the towel along with the reminder: "Use the towel," "Here's the towel," or even playfully, "Remember that towel I brought for you to use?" Midway through the lesson, he stopped himself from wiping across his pants and used the towel on his own! He looked up at me as he did that the first time. I gave him a high five. He used the towel, without checking, every time after that. Again, was it just my words? Of course not, but they are an enormous part of why this worked so easily and quickly.

Let's look at the factors involved in helping Javier change his behavior to what I wanted from him:

1.   I stated what I did want.
2.   I explained why.
3.   I repeated it.
4.   I remained calm, positive, and supportive of his efforts.
5.   I included a physical prompt (offering the towel).

Is twenty minutes a long time to change behaviors for a four-year-old? I don't think so. And the fact that he consistently used the desired behavior for the rest of the one-hour lesson was a great indication that it was sticking. Now, his lessons are a week apart. It's fully possible that when we work on something one week, he won't default to that behavior the next time. But even if he doesn't, my experience tells me it should be relatively easy to bring him back up to speed with it. That's what a learning curve looks like. And this really is the model for working with little kids.

They need to know what is being asked of them, specifically.

They need to know why.

They need help in the form of repeated reminders as they move toward regulating their actions.

And they need those reminders to be calm and supportive while nonetheless holding the line.

Is it tiring? Oh my goodness, yes. But so is cleaning up messes you don't want, day after day. Or feeling frustrated by a kid who won't do what you tell them.

The point is: what we say shapes what kids understand and feel. Taking this kind of approach helps kids build a mental model of what is being asked of them and the internal regulation to be able to follow it through. That takes time. Yelling makes a *big* impression and might stop a behavior in its tracks, but it doesn't do much to ensure that the behavior is actually rewritten.

And using that towel? It took Javier exactly one reminder the following week.

Things to Try

1. The next time you're with a group of children and adults, listen for all the times and ways children are told no. Watch to see what happens. Does it stick?

2. Think of the directives you find yourself repeating to the kids in your life. How could you reword them to make them more effective?

3. The next time you want to tell a child or teen no, try to put what you do want into positive words and offer an explanation.

Two Times Only

As the stories about Javier show, when you're helping a child adapt to a new behavior, it can take a lot of repetition. That takes patience, and you can feel as if you're saying the same thing over and over again.

Yet there are also plenty of times when it's *not* a good idea to repeat yourself—when, in fact, repetition is undermining your efforts and teaching the child exactly the wrong thing. How do you know the difference?

Learning something new takes time, and it takes reminders. But that's only because it's new. It takes kids a while to internalize it. The joke is that it takes a thousand times of saying something for it to go in. It doesn't really take that many, but it can sure feel like it!

When you're trying to get a child's attention, though, it should only take two attempts. Same for when you're asking for something to be done that you know the child knows how to do. You should not find yourself repeatedly making that request.

My rule of thumb for routine situations is that whatever you have to say to a child, say it no more than two times.

Kids are listening all the time. To be fair though, the first time, you might not be heard. So it's OK to try a second time. The second time, you can be sure it was heard. So nonresponse is about something else going on. Know that you are being tested.

If there's physical space between you and the child, there are two ways to bridge that gap: get louder or get closer. Moving in closer is always the better choice. Getting louder just signals that you're losing control. And when we let kids control us, it doesn't lead anywhere good.

Here's an example of why it's a good idea to say something only two times. A five-year-old and his family were out for dinner at a casual family restaurant. Like a lot of children at restaurants these days, the little boy had a smartphone in his hands and was busy playing games. At some point, the mom wanted him to stop and called the boy's name. No answer from the boy, head bent over, rapt attention on the game. She called him again. And again no answer. So she called him again, this time louder, and again and again, getting louder each time. People started looking up from their tables. She called him again. At this point, a relative leaned over to the boy to say, "Your mom is calling you," but the mother shot back that she could manage her own child. She got shrill and called the boy again, *very* loudly. After about fifteen(!) attempts, she snapped out exasperatedly, "Oh never mind!" Only at that point did his little head pop up to ask: "What, Mama?"

Who has whom trained here?

Our words are teaching kids what to think, after all—about us and about themselves. What do you suppose this little guy had already learned?

It's simple to point fingers, and extreme cases like this one are easy targets. But I'd be willing to bet that this mom didn't start out this way—that she wasn't badgering her child when he born. We settle into patterns, all of us. The thing to do is to notice and catch the patterns we see in our own speech. Kids are really resilient. We can start new habits and ways of talking to them at any time. The great news is we really aren't stuck with where we've been. In homes and in classrooms, new norms of speaking *can* be established. It starts with us noticing and choosing to do it differently.

Repeated "requests" are also known as nagging. Two times is all it should take to get your kids to respond to what you need them to do—once to ask, once to remind. And as kids get older, the reminder can go away. I've heard many parents complain to a child or teen, "I've asked you five or six times already!"

Here's the hard news though. If you are "asking" for the fifth or sixth time, there *is* a problem—and it's not with the child. Chapter 8, "Limits and Explanations," will walk you through the steps to take. It may help to remember that repeating the same request isn't helping the child learn to take responsibility for their actions.

Things to Try

1. On your own, decide what you want to do if the second time doesn't work. Families and teachers differ on how they will respond to this. Know before you go into the next interaction how you want to handle noncooperation.

2. The next time your request to a child to do something (or to stop doing something) is ignored, take a breath and remind yourself to ask only one more time. Maintain a calm voice and try again.

3. With older children, try sitting with them at a quiet time and explain that you're going to try something new. Tell them you think two times is enough to have to ask something. Recruit their willingness to do the right thing.

Help Versus Make

Here's one I stumbled on in my own parenting as I was writing this book.

I was describing the follow-up study of the Marshmallow test to my fourteen-year-old son. This test was from a study done by Walter Mischel in the late 1960s (1968–1974). It's fairly widely known now, especially after his book, *The Marshmallow Test*, was published in 2014. Mischel devised a lovely, simple experimental design: four-year-old children attending Bing Nursery School were brought into a room with a table, chair, and a plate with a marshmallow. It was theirs to eat. However, if they waited until the researcher came back, they could have another marshmallow. That was the test. Some kids waited. Many did not. The ones who waited used various strategies to overcome their desire for the marshmallow in front of them.

The study started coming back to public attention when Mischel conducted a major forty-year follow-up in 2009. It's a serendipitous longitudinal study because he hadn't planned to follow up with his young subjects. He describes in the book how his daughter's offhand comments about schoolmates suggested a connection with how those kids had done on the delay test as preschoolers. He felt it was important to start following up, and he did some revisiting once a decade with a sample of the 550 children who took part. The advent of fMRI technology and new interest in brain science led him to a much bigger follow-up.

Forty years is a *long* time from preschool. A lifetime really. Being able to compare whether and how children waited out those agonizing fifteen minutes for that second marshmallow with the paths their lives took later on is really interesting.

Mischel found that on average, the preschoolers who were able to wait out that second marshmallow did better in every major aspect of their lives. By the time they were in their forties, the kids who had waited longer had completed more education, were less likely to use drugs, were less likely to be obese, were more able to pursue their life goals, and reported more resilience and adaptability in their close, important relationships. Who wouldn't want that for their child?

Mischel also describes some of the interim results along the way. In adolescence, the kids who were able to delay their impulse to eat the treat scored higher on the SAT exam and were reported by parents and teachers as having more self-control than their peers, as well as being more robust and mature emotionally, and able to trust themselves more.

More than whether or not they waited, though, Mischel was interested in *how* they waited. What strategies did the kids use?

It turns out that being able to help yourself wait—when what you want is right in front of you but something you want and value even more will come later—serves people really well.

In talking with my fourteen-year-old, I heard myself cast what the kids did as "helping" themselves. I was intrigued (and I think more likely to notice it because I was in the middle of writing this book). When most people talk about self-discipline, there's a lot about *making* yourself do something. That makes sense—the word connotes toughness and rigor and strength. But I had said "helping."

Ask yourself—which would you rather do when confronted with something difficult—*make* yourself or *help* yourself?

And with which do you think you would be more successful?

I think framing the act of self-discipline as self-help rather than self-forcing makes an enormous difference, and I think so especially for children. Children, by definition, are not yet in control of themselves. They have not fully developed their self-regulatory controls, and recent brain-imaging science has suggested that they won't have fully wired the prefrontal cortex needed for such regulation until their mid-twenties, possibly not even at age thirty. So they need help controlling themselves, and they need it for a long time—almost certainly until they are out of your house. We do that for them initially with our bodies: moving them, dressing them, removing things from their reach. And as they grow, we do it increasingly with our words: *wait, no, OK*. Our words. The ones that shape what they think.

Framing acts of self-discipline instead as *helping* yourself does two things:

1.   Casts the act as a skill you can build

2.   Transforms the needed self-discipline into something much friendlier and more doable.

I suspect that many of our smartest (read: "gifted") kids may especially struggle with *making* themselves do things. If your child is "spirited" or "different," this may be an especially useful exercise to try. By simultaneously framing the forward-looking direction of it, and by lowering the bar to success, our words can assist kids in taking action and building their own capacity.

Raising kids isn't like being in the marines. "This recruit" doesn't *have to be* tough to get it done. Especially when "this recruit" is three or seven. Or even fourteen.

It's OK to think about *helping* yourself succeed. This friendlier version is hopeful and optimistic—and after all, it is hope that propels us to action. By tapping into optimism, helping is available each and every time you go back to it. There's less to resist and therefore more likelihood that the child will try. So there's also more likelihood that they will succeed.

Things to Try

1. For a young child having trouble waiting, help them think of one or two things they can do to make waiting easier. Turn the wait into a game—make it playful, and fun, and encourage them to be optimistic about their ability to wait.

2. Start using the word *helping* when you're working with kids. "How can I help?" "Do you want any help with that?" Get into the habit of showing them that you are there and that you believe in their ability to solve their problems.

3. Listen for whether you talk about "making" kids do things they don't want to or whether you voice that idea to them—that they should "make" themselves do something.

6

Positivity First

The strength of positive framing

Have you heard the Cherokee story of the two wolves?

I first heard it about ten years ago and was immediately struck by how broad-reaching its implications were. (There are many versions of this story. The one I think may be the most authoritative is at *firstpeople.us*, a website dedicated to the stories and art of native peoples of the United States and Canada.)

In the version I heard, a young boy and his grandfather are home when two wolves start fighting outside. The sound is loud and terrible, and the boy is frightened. His grandfather tells him the wolves fight there every night. It is their way.

He tells his grandson that it is the same for people. There are two wolves inside each of us, one good and one evil.

The boy thinks about it and then asks his elder, "Which one will win, Grandfather?"

His answer? "The one you feed."

Feeding negativity breeds negativity. In this chapter, we'll see how speaking in a way that accentuates the positive shapes children's thinking for the better.

Framing Things Positively

Have you ever been around someone who continually brings things down to a negative viewpoint, who can't seem to see anything going right? They're not fun to be around. And have you ever been around the opposite: someone who is perennially cheery and makes the best of everything that happens, no matter what? I don't know about you, but I find this kind of person kind of grating.

Luckily, this chapter isn't about an artificial contrast between being negative versus being chirpy. It's about framing the world in ways that are positive and that align with your goals, as opposed to focusing on what you don't want in the world. That framing can make a world of difference.

Take the experience of one South Bronx principal trying to improve her school as part of New York City's Renewal School Program. Principal Alison Coviello described the program this way in a 2017 *Hechinger Report* article: "It was the first time at this school that anyone came with the lens of 'What's going well and how can we support it?' instead of looking for what's wrong. The paradigm of support instead of shutting down—it's huge. I can't even put into words what it did for us and our morale.'"

This idea that your outlook can influence your outcome can sound either mystical or practical, depending on the delivery. New age folks call it "manifesting": the idea that you draw to yourself whatever you focus on. Meditation and yoga experts say that "prana follows awareness"; in other words, energy flows wherever the attention goes. Sports coaches just point out that the ball's going to go wherever you're looking.

No matter what flavor you give it, this idea is important. It's another powerful way where what we say to kids shapes what they think. When we use a positive framing, we help children construct a world in which they are agents and they have the power to make what they want happen. And it comes in everywhere, even in small ways like these:

POSITIVE FRAMING	NEGATIVE FRAMING
"I want to stay warm."	"I don't want to get cold."
"Let's play this one."	"That one's not fun."
"We need to wait."	"We don't get to go yet." (or even "It's not our turn.")
"Strengthening your joints."	"Not hurting yourself."

I first encountered this idea from the perspective of a parent during graduate school, when my daughter started at her extraordinary daycare, the Children's Center for the Stanford Community (completely separate from the well-known Bing Nursery School on campus). CCSC is not a lab school, it's a full-day daycare center for ages eight weeks to five years. The teachers at every age group practice a sort of relentless optimism. Their perspective is that it creates a positive outlook and thus a more capable kid. It is terrific early training for the children who go to the center.

And because it's a parent participation daycare, we parents were inadvertently trained as well. I found it life changing to view the world in this way, and it became part of how we talked at home. The language used by the teachers seeped into the kids, who were getting it natively, after all (just like the language used at the elementary school my kids attended).

My friend Karen has the most hilarious example of this, from a time she took her four-year-old son Josh to their local library. Little Josh was deeply engaged in playing on the iPad there, since he didn't have access to one at home. As he was playing, another child came over to look. This boy kept reaching over and trying to touch the screen, but Josh kept playing quietly. Just as my friend was wondering whether she should step in to help her son, Josh looked up at the other little boy. He calmly moved this boy's hand away as he said, "No thank you. I don't need your help right now. You can use it when I'm done." Then he quietly went back to playing! Karen burst out laughing as she recounted this story and asked me, "What four-year-old talks like that?" Then we both blurted out at the same time, "A CCSC kid!"

Framing in a positive way, then, is an extension of the idea of not saying no. In not saying no, the point is to phrase what is needed of the child/teen in a way that clearly articulates what the desired behavior is. That helps them follow through on it.

In putting things in a positive frame, we're going further. We're casting the world in the way we want it to be: active, interesting, patient, etc.

I'm not suggesting you live in a fantasy. This isn't about wish fulfillment. It's about actually living in the small moments in life, with purpose and in a way that makes life better. Small moments stacked together become our life. If we focus on what we want to have happen, it's easier to work toward it and bring it about.

Positivity and the Brain

This isn't always easy. Like not saying no, if you haven't been raised speaking this way, it's unfamiliar and can be uncomfortable. That's where another popular idea can help:

Fake it til you make it. New brain science is reinforcing what coaches have known for a long time: attitude matters. If you can't have a good attitude, act as if you do and it will come eventually.

The brain science is also clear that focusing on negative thoughts takes us no place good. It bathes us in the equivalent of neurochemistry stress soup. At a functional level, being focused on negative thoughts actually *slows down brain-processing* speeds. That's why when you're upset, it's harder to put your thoughts together and harder to find a positive solution to a problem.

This is again where "neurons that fire together, wire together" comes in. From a neuroscience perspective, we are, absolutely, what we pay attention to. If what we practice in our thoughts and in our speech has a negative slant on the world, that will become the default lens through which we process what happens to us. The great news out of neuroscience in the past decade is the extent to which neuroplasticity allows us to reshape the brain. And getting a head start on the brain while it is still under development—in other words, during childhood or adolescence—means that the changes are more likely to stick and become permanently wired in.

Here's an odd but simple exercise for you to try. Bite across a pencil and open your mouth as wide as you can. Actually try it.

The brain is tricked by the physical sensation of "smiling," and you do actually feel happier afterward. I was introduced to this idea during graduate school. It stems from experimental work done in the 1980s on what's known as the *facial feedback hypothesis.* Our facial expressions don't just mirror or express our feelings. They also *shape* our feelings.

Body–mind–body. It's a loop. The good news is we can enter it at any point and nudge the system to a better place. It's critical we understand, though, that language—the stuff we hear and the stuff we tell ourselves silently inside our heads—plays a huge part in how we approach the world:

"I can't get to sleep."

"I'm never going to be able to finish this homework."

"I'm dead. My dad is going to kill me for this."

These are thoughts that are *not* going to help kids dig themselves out of a hole. But they do address real problems kids have, and no amount of sweet, positive wording is going to remove that fact.

So how do we help kids take the negative and reframe it? What would it look like to spin these into something that focuses more on a positive frame of reference?

I've always disliked the response "It'll all be OK." In my head I rebut with, "How would you know?" or even just "How?" I know that people say it from a place of well-meaning and wanting to reassure. But it neither addresses the root of the person's problem, nor does it tackle how they can solve it. For me, it just comes across as empty words.

Bad things do and will happen. As children grow, they face real and painful difficulties. Positive framing is about more than empty words. It's about building one's world with a belief that hardship can be overcome. Positive framing helps you recruit others to help, or it calls on deeper inner resources.

"I'm having trouble falling asleep. Got any ideas?"

"I have so much homework I don't know how to get it done."

"I'm really scared about what my parents are going to say."

Positive framing is about not accepting the negative events and feelings as the permanent reality. You can see them for what they are: temporary and surmountable.

And the great news is: this can be taught.

Building Positivity

Martin Seligman, often cited as the founder of positive psychology, studies optimism and well-being. Like Walter Mischel in *The Marshmallow Test*, Seligman believes that the skills needed to live well—skills like self-control and optimism—can be taught. His book *The Optimistic Child* (1995, 2007) has a whole chapter looking at the sources and origins of optimism. Of course, genetics plays a part. By his calculation, though, less than half of a person's measured optimism can be explained through family, or heritable, traits. That means *more* than half of it is learned—at home, on the sports field, and at school.

The whole purpose behind *The Optimistic Child* is to show how Seligman's research can be, and has been, put into effect in schools. In these programs, children are expressly taught about the difference between optimism and pessimism, and taught how to identify the kinds of thoughts that are more negative.

That this can be successfully instructed—typically with middle-school students—is well documented. As of 2005, eleven replication studies had been done to test his work, and eight of them corroborated the success of the programs. That's a huge success rate in research done with people.

And those other three studies didn't actually *disprove* his work; they were merely inconclusive. Seligman points out that these three studies all shared one common feature: they gave short shrift to the training of the teachers. Everyone working in education understands that teacher professional training is the key to good implementation. Inadequate teacher training could very easily impact the chances of the program succeeding. Taken together, these eleven studies offer overwhelming support for his main point that these skills are learnable.

The longitudinal studies (studies done with the same subjects repeatedly over a period of time) also document the *limits* of the program. Even with young, neuroplastic brains, one program is not enough to forever rewrite the brain. The children taking part in Seligman's programs appear to have a good two years of benefit. Beyond that, without additional input, the gains fade out.

Throughout the book, Seligman discusses the benefits to children of being more optimistic. Pessimism is strongly linked to depression, and Seligman is blunt in saying that his optimism programs "depression-proof" kids. In addition to depression, pessimism is also associated with having poor *physical* health, with underachievement generally, and with resignation and disengagement versus working to better one's life. Optimism—the opposite of pessimism—protects against these outcomes.

Because Seligman is convinced that the skill of optimism can be learned, he focuses on thoughts and from there, on talk. He zeroes in on what he calls people's *explanatory style*—in other words, what they tell themselves about the cause of what is happening to them. Seligman shows how this kind of self-talk really shapes how we feel about the world. He then points out that children learn their explanatory style largely from their parents—from what they hear day in and day out in how their parents interpret the world.

Roughly speaking, explanatory styles are either positive or negative. A positive outlook involves seeing setbacks as temporary, as specific instances of failure, and as originating in the environment, or outside the individual. A negative outlook flips all of these—setbacks are framed and understood more rigidly, as unchangeable or permanent problems, that seep into other areas or are pervasive, and point to a failure of the person's character.

Laid out like this, it's easy to understand that having a positive outlook feels better. Seligman's point is that it doesn't just *feel* better—it creates the space to learn better, live more healthfully, and succeed more.

One of the central pieces to Seligman's training for kids involves training *parents* to see their own explanatory style and then how to catch themselves when they use a negative style. Because, as Seligman points out, "Children are sponges, they soak up both what you say and how you say it" (2007, 162).

That's what I mean when I talk about creating a positive outlook or about being relentlessly optimistic. It's not about an all-is-good-in-the-world outlook. It's about framing the bad stuff in ways that make room for hope, for change, and for optimism.

As we saw at the beginning of the book, even the smallest word change from *but* to *and* can shift the meaning of what we say. And as we saw in the last chapter, telling children what you *do* want versus what you don't helps them visualize and internalize the actions you want them to learn.

When we put things in a positive frame, we help children build that frame *internally*. Here's a simple example.

Remember versus Don't forget

Being prompted to remember what they need to do casts kids in a positive direction. It positions them for success, and it helps them build an inner capacity for responsible action.

Think of the problem this way: what is it you want for the child? For them to recall on their own.

What is it you don't want? For them to forget.

So it's helpful to ask, which of these two actions are you prompting for them? Think of this literally—which one are your words calling up in their mind?

Putting things in a positive framing is about this very feature of human beings and our language use. Whatever we practice becomes stronger. If we practice the negative outcome—in this case, forgetting—we increase our chances of performing it.

Keeping in mind the longitudinal research on Seligman's optimism program, we have to remember that one burst of positive framing won't be enough all by itself. That's a lot of what inspires me to write this. If we start practicing using our words differently now, we can learn to get better at it. If we begin to tune our attention to using language with kids more positively, we give them a stronger foundation.

Our words, à la Vygotsky and the idea of internalization, are the building blocks kids use to form their regulation of their actions. Let's give them the ones that will help them succeed!

Things to Try

1. It's entirely possible to think of ourselves as positive people and yet slip into speaking negatively or griping. Run a check on yourself for a day. How many negative sounding things come out of your mouth? Are you surprised? What would you want to do differently?

2. The next time you're talking with a child, listen for ways that you can flip what you're saying to a more positive frame or perspective. Try at least one.

3. If framing positively is easy for you, listen carefully to what the kids (and other adults) in your life sound like. How could you support them in reframing? For young children, it works really well to simply say what you want them to say and have them repeat it after you. For teens, you need to take a more nuanced approach. If possible, draw them into a conversation about this section of the book and ask their opinion.

Positive First, Correction After

People are funny beings. We like to hear nice things about ourselves. Even for thick-skinned, ardently growth-minded individuals, criticism can sometimes feel harsh.

Maybe you've seen the phrase "connect, then redirect" in parenting circles or on classroom walls. And yes, that's accomplished if you hit the positive first. But what I'm suggesting is more than this. Because the positive here isn't just about establishing a warm connection. It's about shaping a child's or teen's understanding of the world.

When giving feedback—whether in a professional setting, in a classroom, or at home—it really helps to say something positive *first*. Then go for the constructive comment about what needs attention. Note that *constructive* doesn't allow for insults. Feedback isn't shaming, and it isn't as simple as criticizing.

In the art and performance world, there is a difference between *criticism*, which attacks, and *critique*, which evaluates what's working and what isn't. What I'm suggesting here is closer to critique. If we have something we need kids to change/work on/improve, *they* and *we* are better served when we come at it from this angle.

How we structure what we say around feedback is integral to how kids will hear it and ultimately to how they will use it to think about themselves and their work.

An elementary school example

Students at Mulberry School start learning how to give feedback on their classmates' work during third grade. By fourth grade, such feedback is codified as "gems and rocks." A *gem* is a favorable comment or compliment. A *rock* is a comment about something that could be improved or didn't work. The rule is: "You can't give a rock without first giving a gem." Simple. And oh so difficult. In today's web-enabled, TED-talk world, even nine-year-olds are sophisticated audience members. They can tell when something isn't well-organized, or when you don't make eye contact, when you're rushing, or when you're too quiet to be heard. They can tell. And they want to let you know about it!

Training these fourth graders to *first* say something real that is favorable tunes their attention and their empathy. They end up on the receiving end of these comments eventually and realize just how important it is to hear something nice first. They have to organize their thoughts and to find something genuine to compliment. It's a lot of work, and it takes time in the classroom. The result, though, is that these kids learn to make better presentations, and they also learn how to give effective feedback.

A parenting example

One morning, I went to use our blender and couldn't find the lid. The night before, my teenaged son had asked me if it went in the dishwasher, so I knew it was around somewhere. I looked on the counter, in the sink, in the dishwasher (yes, I checked to make sure). It wasn't with the blender or in the cabinet where the other appliances are kept. I was stumped.

I have to be honest—I was feeling a bit frustrated. I was short on time and I had looked in several obvious (to me) places. Mornings can be a bit frenzied in many homes. Maybe you've had moments like this and also wondered, how can a teenager not know where something goes?

I had a choice to make in how I spoke to him. I could have pounced on him. I could have simply asked where the lid was.

Keep in mind that what I wanted to build was his sense of competent independence. I wanted him to feel capable and good about the work he had done the night before, rather than leave him feeling chastised for doing something wrong.

I know that my words shape what he thinks and feels. So how could I use a moment like this to reinforce what I wanted him to learn? Here's what I went with: "Thanks for cleaning up the dishes last night. Where did you end up putting the lid to the blender?"

He laughed. He said he'd had to think about where to put it. It turned out he *had* put it in the cabinet with the appliances— disassembled and on a different shelf. I had missed it in my search. Now imagine how I would have felt if I'd come down heavy on him! While this incident may seem small, thousands like it are what build our children's view of themselves.

How important is this?

I've heard various "ratios" about how many good things you need to say for every negative one in order to build and maintain positive relationships with kids or other adults. I've heard 3:1, 5:1, and even 10:1—it's hard to imagine managing that! I've most often heard it referred to as "banking." The idea is that you want to deposit those good interactions—especially with your teenagers—so that when the inevitable bad stuff happens, it still balances out to be positive.

Turns out there is research on this.

Barbara Fredrickson is one of the world's foremost researchers on positive psychology. She and her colleague Marcela Losado came up with what they call the Losado Ratio for positivity. Positivity matters, of course. We can all understand that. But it turns out *how much positivity* one experiences matters even more. Using data they collected on business groups and on individuals, Fredrickson and Losado were able to show that there is a tipping point in whether or not positivity leads to thriving, what they call *flourishing*. That ratio is 2.9:1. That means it takes almost three times more positive interactions than negative interactions to result in a good outcome. That's three positive moments for every negative moment, on average.

In her 2009 book *Positivity*, Fredrickson describes the complex mathematics behind the ratio and links it to other social science researchers' work. She points first to the work of well-known marriage researcher John Gottman. From his decades of work, Gottman has found that couples who have a 5:1 ratio of positive to negative interactions are vastly more likely to thrive and remain together than are couples with lower ratios. Fredrickson also discusses the work of clinical psychologist Robert Schwartz, whose research into the impact of various treatments on depression found that a 4:1 ratio is necessary for well being. Frederickson finds that the ratio shows up at roughly the same range in various kinds of research. There's something important going on here.

Neuropsychologist Rick Hanson also backs up the idea of a ratio and needing to hit the positive more often. He explains it in terms of what's called the brain's *negativity bias*. Human brains have evolved to be careful of threat, and so our brains scan for, notice, and lock onto negative stimuli more readily than the positive stuff.

When we have something negative to talk about, it really helps defuse the feeling of being attacked to start with something positive. Not just any nice thing will work of course. It has to be genuine and relevant. Like with gems and rocks. Learning to take this approach will help people of all ages hear what you want them to.

Things to Try

1. Get an idea of your own Losado Ratio. Start by tracking how many positive things you say to the kids in your life. If you have more than one child at home, or thirty-plus in a classroom, you might make a quick chart. I'd suggest focusing on one child at a time, even if only for brief interactions.

2. Build some empathy. Listen for how much the people in your life use positive messages with you. Notice how you feel when they do and when they don't.

3. Practice. The next time you need to offer feedback—on chores, on classwork, or whatever—think about what you want the child to learn from you. What can you sincerely offer as a positive reflection first, before giving any corrective information/advice?

Being Real, and Positive

When I say things like "not saying no" or "putting things in a positive framing," you might think I'm advocating being soft. Far from it.

What I advocate is being real. And within that, finding a way to be positive.

Here's an example. I've been doing yoga for about twelve years. It keeps me healthy, and it keeps me sane. Yoga classes often include people with a wide range of skills. Teachers often need to show a progression of steps in a pose—from an entry level to deeper and more complicated versions of the pose. At all times, good teachers remind the class to pay attention to *their body* and do what is right for their body *today*—not what's happening on someone else's mat or what they were able to do in class last week. It's clear that this is a struggle for many students, especially beginners. Many yoga students feel tremendous pressure to "do the pose right" or do it as well as the people around them.

The Easy Way

In class recently, my yoga teacher referred to the initial version of a very complicated twisting pose as "the easy way." I was surprised—it seemed so *un*-politically correct to just blatantly point out that you might be at the lowest level. Gradually, though, I was able to see the deeper intent behind what he was saying. It *was* the easy version, after all. And that's the message he was conveying to his students—that we need to be real with ourselves about where our bodies are. If we are at the easy version, so be it. Our kids need this message too.

Too often, with today's self-esteem movement and not wanting kids to get discouraged, we buffer the language we use. Nothing is hard anymore; it's "challenging." What's wrong with not being able to do something? With not being great yet? What's wrong with being at the starting point? Nothing. Let's be real about where we are—with ourselves and with our kids.

Competitive Sports

Being real and also being positive doesn't mean being soft. The world of competitive sports offers a great example. This idea —that what we say influences what kids think—is the very foundation of an organization that's doing great work in sports. Positive Coaching Alliance (PCA), founded in 1998, is on a mission to transform kids' sports and the culture that's brought us cheating, arrogance, and bullying. Their work is "to transform the youth sports culture into a Development Zone where all youth and high school athletes have a positive, character-building experience that results in better athletes, better people."

I was introduced to this organization by my daughter's elementary school physical education teacher. She had found and gone through the Positive Coaching Alliance training. At the time, PCA was fairly new and just starting to reach broader awareness. As I looked over their materials back then, I was impressed. The message was very on point, consistent with what I knew about kids, and was definitely needed in the world.

PCA has grown a lot. Their results are immediately apparent—in changed school culture, kids' behavior on- and off-field, and in the terms that matter most in sports—winning. Check their website now, and you'll find endorsements from major US professional team heads. Their National Advisory

Board is filled with Olympic athletes; head coaches of national teams; and professors like Albert Bandura, the pioneer of understanding how role modeling works, and Carol Dweck, of growth mindset fame.

The reason for all the support? What Positive Coaching Alliance does is retrain coaches and athletes to think differently about what they're doing. They teach kids to value their mistakes and to respect themselves, their teammates, their competitors, and the game. The language they use in their trainings is all geared to help athletes and coaches redefine their ideas of good sportsmanship. It's meant to translate into healthier, more positive self-talk for the athletes later. And it does.

Here's an example from their external evaluations. In a survey of middle school students in Dallas whose coaches went through the program, three hundred eighty-six kids across eleven different schools responded.

- Over three-fourths of the kids (78 percent) said they had learned to use specific tools to recover from mistakes in the game. This included positive redirection, like "mistakes are OK."

- These kids were overwhelming likely (88 percent) to believe that their sports ability "could grow and was limitless," and about three-quarters of the kids who thought this (76 percent) said the PCA program had influenced that belief.

- Three-quarters of these middle school kids (76 percent) reported getting better at "encouraging their teammates to stay positive if a bad call was made."

- Two-thirds of the kids reported feeling more positively toward the game officials after the training.

The bottom line message from Positive Coaching Alliance is that "encouraging athletes with positive reinforcement helps them hear and heed the necessary corrections. With that winning combination of truthful, specific praise and constructive criticism, athletic performance improves and so do the chances that kids stick with sports longer and learn all the valuable life lessons inherently available through organized competition."

It is not just outward-facing advice to the kids. As an organization, they operate under what they call "a relentless commitment to continual improvement." Winning takes hard work, sustained over time.

If everything is easy, nothing is really that worth doing.

So yes, some things are hard. That's just reality. Kids really are up to hearing that. They won't buckle under the supposed weight of that reality. When we know it's going to be hard, we can set our expectations accordingly. We can tell ourselves, "I have to keep trying. This will take time. I can get this eventually."

No empty words here. Just plain common sense.

Things to Try

1. Identify where you fall on the continuum of positive = soft. If that's an issue for you, consider how you can shift that belief.

2. Consider what strengths you can build for children when you accept where you are and stay positive about moving toward better performance.

3. The next time you're working with a child who is feeling defeated by poor performance, help the child see a value to their mistake and how working with it can help them get closer to their goals.

7

The Power of Questions

Understanding and self-regulation

Adults don't tend to ask kids what they think. It's always amazing to me. Children have minds, after all. But we don't credit them with being able to think for themselves. Or worse, we don't expect that anything they could think of would be very useful. I'm not immune to this. I sometimes catch myself doing things for my kids when it would serve them better to ask them what they need or think. It's often when we're in a rush or when I'm feeling pressed for time. I try to stay aware so I can catch myself.

There are so many benefits to asking children before telling them: questions invite deeper thought and support better memory, and they help children learn to self-regulate. The type of questions we ask also makes a difference.

Asking Versus Telling

Having to answer a question activates a different part of our thinking than listening does. Listening is rather passive, after all. Answering requires a more active effort in the conversation.

Questions come in two basic forms: *closed-ended questions*, which require a simple answer from a narrow, presupposed range of possibilities (most often a simple yes-or-no answer) and *open-ended questions*, which allow for any sort of answer of any length. Research is clear that open-ended questions build children's thinking.

Part of this is because children trust that adults know what they're talking about. If we tell kids something, that becomes the basis for their understanding. If we ask them something, though, children have to come up with the basis for their understanding. That's more difficult cognitively—and more powerful.

A terrific example is a simple and tightly constructed 2011 study by Daphna Buchsbaum, Alison Gopnik, and colleagues. They introduced a new and complex toy to four- and five-year-olds, either by musing "I wonder how this toy works?" or by saying "I'm going to show you how my toy works." The children were then handed the toy to play with. The preschoolers who were told how the toy works heavily reproduced the demonstrated moves. The preschoolers who were asked the open-ended question explored the toy freely, in novel ways, and longer. We think we're helping by telling children all the time. What we really need to be doing is asking more.

There's more. Do you want your child or students to be able to remember things better? Ask them more open-ended questions during an event. It will enhance their memory later.

Asking kids questions also gets them to figure out what they already know but aren't focused on. It's a great way to help children remind *themselves*, rather than you having to be the one to remind them directly.

When I was growing up, our next-door neighbor and dear friend Pat was a first-grade teacher. She used to let me come help out when she was setting up her classroom at the start of the year, unpacking the boxes and setting up the learning stations. I loved sorting out all the things she organized in little boxes for her students: Cuisinaire rods for math or beads and paper for art. Her room always felt warm and welcoming, and I loved hearing her talk about her students. It was clear that she loved teaching.

Talking with Pat about this book and about how what we say shapes how kids think, she chuckled and told me this story. Whenever she found one of her first graders wandering around the classroom, she asked them a question rather than telling them where they needed to be. Pat laughed as she recalled it. "I would ask them, 'Where are you *supposed* to be?' And they would look at me as if to say, 'Oh no. My *teacher* doesn't even know where I'm supposed to be. Where *am* I supposed to be?' and then they would scurry off over to the right place!"

Asking children does two things, at minimum: it engages their problem-solving efforts, and it signals that we take them seriously. Both are necessary for children to develop their problem-solving capacity.

So when something goes wrong, ask the child what they think. It's really that simple. And also that hard. For many of us it requires a complete switch of gears, or mindset. How one asks, of course, varies by the child's age. Some examples:

At three, perhaps, "What should we do?"

At nine, "What do you think needs to happen?"

At fourteen, "What's the downside?"

There is one big exception: if there's bleeding or a colossal mess, tend to that first. The talking can always wait! But do get back around to it.

The question "Why is that important to you?" works well with teens. It has to be asked in a genuine way though—no snarking allowed or the tone will undo the power of the words.

Here's an example. When our son was almost fifteen, he took on a heavy course load at school and also landed a role in the fall school play. Just as he was beginning a new school year, he fell into a very full schedule.

He handled it pretty gracefully for the most part. He was on top of what homework was due and when. He enjoyed the rehearsal and theater time, kept up with his piano practice, and even fit in his soccer practices and weekly game pretty easily. A few things did drop, though. One of those was doing his chores.

We have family meetings, and I had already brought chores to one of our meetings in an attempt to double down on getting them done. No success. Time for a new approach. I sat down with just my teenager and asked, "So, chores. What's happening here do you think?"

We all knew he wasn't getting to them, so there was no need for him to deflect it. He trusted that I was genuinely opening a conversation, not waiting to nail him, and so he started talking. That's key: he knew that I would actually be listening to him.

He told me that he was so focused on the schoolwork, and it was often so late when he got home, that he just wanted some time on the piano and not to *have* to do anything. And that on the days he was supposed to do his chores, by the time he'd eaten dinner, he had forgotten about them.

He then suggested a new plan: it would be easier to remember his chores if there were one or two to do each day rather than a stack of them on only a couple days a week. Then he went and got an index card to write them down. We sat together, going through his list of chores for the week, discussing when each one made the most sense, both for the family's needs and given his schedule. No yelling, no fighting, no conflict. Forward-looking, solution-oriented work.

If you think my son is some kind of anomaly—or alien creature—you're wrong. He is a very normal teenage boy who is messy and loud, at times surly and argumentative. He's also wonderful and conscientious and fun. He is who he is. But he is both willing—and able—to engage in this kind of problem-solving endeavor. He feels capable of thinking for himself and coming up with solutions that work for him.

Do you wonder if the new system worked flawlessly? Of course it didn't. The good news is that's not the point anyway. The bigger point is that in making progress on growing this child, we have helped him to a point where he can seek and build his own solutions, with people he cares about, in a way that will work for both sides. I'm pretty happy about that. And I'm willing to take some messy counters along the way.

Things to Try

1. For an elementary school child who is struggling to get work done (chores, homework, etc.), ask how you can help. Then listen to their ideas.

2. For a young child who is feeling intense emotion (sadness, anger), ask them how they feel. If they can't put it into words, say how it looks to you and ask if that's right. Let them find their own words, even if it's a bit of a struggle.

3. For teenagers, try asking what they think about something you know matters to them—whether that's the latest YouTube phenomenon or a club at high school. Not sure what matters to your teen? No time like the present to ask them! "So what's the latest thing in your world?"

Cueing Self-Regulation

In chapter 5 I talked about asking children two times only, saying repeated requests mean there is a problem, and it's not with the child. That's kind of right and kind of wrong. Repeated requests *are* a problem: the adult isn't managing the situation effectively. There's also an underlying problem, and that lies with the child.

Anytime you hear yourself reminding the same thing, time after time, that's the signal that there is a regulation issue. It's time to switch from telling to asking.

This may seem counterintuitive. The kid isn't managing well, even with your support. How are they supposed to manage if you don't remind them? Isn't it clear that they need your help?

The answer is yes. But the issue here is that the reminders aren't sticking. You can tell, and tell, and tell again. But at this point you're simply a crutch. A prop that, when you pull it out, leaves the kid falling over. You need to build their ability to stand on their own without you. And to do that, you need to take a completely different approach.

Remember: what we say shapes how kids think. We're looking to use our words in ways that will help kids build the knowledge and skills they need to be successfully independent.

Transition times are an example. Parents, teachers and after-school providers all face this problem. At home, mornings can be crazy bad, especially if there are young kids or kids with any kind of attentional or behavioral issues. Even good parents can end up yelling in the morning to get the kids out the door on time.

Time after time I found myself—politely but teeth gritted—reminding my twelve-year-old son to get his things, to put a lunch together, or to have his sports stuff for practice after school.

I finally heard myself.

I started asking instead, "What do you need to be ready?"

Shifting from telling to asking is about shifting the child into regulating their own actions. In my example, that's remembering the things they need *and* making sure that they have them ready to go. It requires that the adult back out a bit to make room for the child to step in to fill the void. The catch is there's no single prescription for how far to step out.

It's OK to let children flail a bit. Of course we don't want them to struggle beyond their capability. But our current sense of needing to make sure everything is OK for kids is not helping them build a sense of independence and capability. In fact, we're stripping them of those things in the name of making them comfortable. Asking kids to think through what they need to manage (lunch boxes, backpacks, clearing up a desk before outside playtime) builds their internal model of how that step goes and what they are responsible for completing.

Not sure how to work this? Here's a possible progression for helping kids get ready in the morning. Take a look at the sequence on the next page. Do you see the shift in self-regulation that happens with each line?

"Get your sports stuff."

        Parent tells the child what to do so that it gets done—maybe

"Do you have your sports stuff?"

      Simple shift from telling outright to question version of the same thing

"Do you have what you need for after school?"

                  Reminder to think about the end of the day;

        implies there's something they need without explicitly saying sports

"Do you need anything for after school?"

                        Cues to think about after school

                  without implying that the answer is yes

"What do you need to have with you today?"

                  Very general—cues child to think through the day,

                      either with you or alone

"Do you have everything you need today?"

      For an older child/teen, cues them to go through a mental checklist

Let's break it down. When telling the child what to get, the parent is regulating the whole situation by helping the child:

1. Remember that there is sports today

2. Remember, therefore, that sports stuff is needed

3. Monitor whether the sports stuff is ready

When spelled out like this, hopefully, you can see that it is madness to be the keeper of all this information for each child in your charge, for every aspect of what they need to remember. It's no wonder so many parents and teachers are exhausted. This level of constant load on our working memories and attentional systems is exhausting. In fact, the sooner you can shift kids into successfully regulating for themselves, the sooner everyone will be happier.

In the example progression above, the parent is pulling out a little bit of support at each step. So take another look at the list above and then go back through the example to see what piece of regulation is being shifted to the child at each step.

Some of the best early research in my field was done on apprenticeships. It marked a huge shift from what was considered important enough for psychological research. In her now-classic 1988 book *Cognition in Practice*, Jean Lave presented her study of apprentices in five different domains. What she found was that how the apprenticeship was organized mattered greatly. Weavers in Guatemala, for example, had a slow steady progression in what they were allowed to be in charge of. Over time, they learned the whole process and became adept enough to go out on their own. Apprenticed butchers in US supermarkets, though, got pigeon-holed. They only ever got to do the grunt work, while the master butchers did the "real" work. These apprentices never actually learned all the tricks of their trade.

So go back to the morning routines for a moment. Why doesn't it work to remind kids each morning to get their stuff?

It makes sense, doesn't it, that whether or not the stuff is ready is actually the easiest piece to do? And that's the secret. When we're stuck in telling mode, we actually focus the child's attention on that easiest layer of regulation. So that simplest layer is the only piece the child ever gets exposure to and practice in. Like the butcher apprentices, our kids aren't ever being asked to take responsibility for the bigger, less obvious pieces of work. They aren't practicing getting better at it. So it is unlikely that they will.

This is the secret behind why kids often don't assume more responsibility for their things. We literally aren't asking them to.

What we say shapes what they think. If we don't ask them to think about it for themselves, they aren't likely to start on their own. But if we throw them in the deep end and tell them to manage the whole process on their own before they're ready, they aren't likely to succeed. It takes steps, and effort. It's worth it though: Not having to be the external memory and gatekeeper for everything will keep you sane!

Things to Try

1. Look for the places where you're repeating the same prompts over and over. Which step in the progression does this correspond to?

2. Think about how you can reword your reminder as a question. (Use the questions in the progression above as examples.) Try that for the next couple of days.

3. When you think you see progress in the child's ability to work at this new level, bump to the next one.

Known-Answer Questions

Asking has its limits, however. It depends a lot on what kinds of questions you ask. In classrooms and in educated middle- and upper-middle-class homes, the questions children get the most are what are called "known-answer" questions.

- What color is that boat?
- What comes next after three?
- What does the cow say?

Without any doubt, the adult asking these knows the answer. These are more prompts than they are genuine questions. So there is no actual discovery or true conversation happening. Instead, this is a performative type of question in which one side (the child) does or does not cough up the right answer. Imagine if your best friend talked to you this way when you got together for coffee!

Kids come into these "conversations" understanding the part they are to play. It can be fun at times—I'm not saying it's all bad. But these conversations aren't really deep or meaningful. Let's also ask what these questions teach children.

Recall that any time we interact with kids we can ask, "What am I teaching in this moment?" The lessons a child is learning can be about:

- Him/herself
- Me as a parent/teacher/adult
- What our family/school/group values are
- Life

So with known-answer questions, what are children learning?

First, since the answer is supposed to be known, the child is only rehearsing what they know. They're not actually building any new knowledge. So the purpose here is not about them adding new material, but about the child performing it so that the adult can assess what they know. Parents often ask these questions when they have another adult with them. The performative aspect here is very clear, especially to the child being prompted.

But keep in mind that kids are actively learning at all times. Given that there isn't new *content* to learn, the child's learning focus shifts to the *interaction* itself.

Second, since the answer is known and the child is just being tested, this kind of interaction sets up the expectation that the adult is someone who tests and the child is someone who is tested. Children learn quickly that they are to show off their knowledge or to perform on demand. They also learn whether they are seen as good at this or as a disappointment.

In the classroom, this format for questioning is so well-recognized it even has a name: Initiation-Response-Evaluation (IRE). (In England, it's IRF, for Feedback). This structure was first written about in the 1970s, but it is still the most prevalent form of teacher-student talk in US classrooms. Which is a shame really, since it doesn't teach kids much when we ask them questions they and we already know the answers to.

Children are very quick to learn the format for social interactions. And classrooms have rules for acceptable participation—some explicit and others unspoken. You have to raise your hand if you want to talk. You have to ask to leave to go to the bathroom. (Nowhere else do we expect this kind of behavior, yet we understand that in classrooms it is expected and required. To the point where even some of my college students will ask if they need to leave the room.)

What researchers John Sinclair and Malcolm Coulthard in England, and Bud Mehan in the United States were able to show is that the same is true for how we talk. Classrooms are organized in ways that create patterns, and these patterns reflect what the teacher considers important. IRE/IRF interactions are about assessment, not about learning. The teacher or parent is checking to see if the child or class knows the answer. There are times when this is both valuable and necessary; you'd like to be sure before you move on. But for this to be the bulk of how we talk to kids doesn't help them build much new of value. Instead, when teachers ask questions that require deeper thinking, make connections, or form new questions, students engage with the material more and actually learn more.

Things to Try

1. Listen for when you (or others around you) prompt a child to give a known answer. How does the child seem to feel about the interaction?

2. When you catch yourself asking a known-answer question, see if you can dig for a deeper question as well. What might spark the child's genuine interest or curiosity about the topic?

3. Ask the children you interact with to describe something they are interested in. Listen to the way they talk about things that matter to them. Compare that to how they sound when answering a known-answer question.

8

Limits and Explanations

Why, when, and how

I remember being stunned by a story my mom told me when I was in high school. My grandmother, an elegant woman, was visited by a friend and her two-year-old son. During the visit, the boy crawled on the floor, and began biting my grandmother's shoe! After a minute of this, the mother finally told him, "Johnny, if you don't stop, I'm simply going to have to say no."

Apparently, it took every shred of my grandmother's self-restraint not to give little Johnny a small kick right to the teeth!

Discipline is *always* a touchy subject with parents. It's a safe assumption that every parent wants the best for their child and is highly invested in bringing up their child well. So telling a parent he or she is doing it wrong is tantamount to a personal attack.

And yet, clearly, parents do things that don't work.

This chapter looks at setting limits for kids: how we do it, what we say, and how that shapes what kids understand and do.

Setting Limits

For starters, it's important to give *all* kids limits, even babies. Things like:

> *"I can't let you do that."*

"Two more times, then it's her turn."

"You can play video games after you finish your homework."

Limits are the conditions we set for kids about the behavior that we will accept. They help kids understand what is wanted from them. They're parameters; they establish a sort of zone of clarity and certainty. There's no magic formula for setting a limit; it can specify what kids can and can't do, when they can do it, or what will happen if they do/don't. The point is that they clarify the expectation.

My students are often surprised when I explain that kids need, and actually want, limits. Knowing where they stand helps kids do the right thing. And as research on *effortful control* shows us, for the most part kids really do want to cooperate.

It also surprises my students when I say to give babies limits. They're confused: babies can't control themselves; why would you give them limits? Here's the thing:

1. Babies *can* control themselves, a little.

2. It gets them, and you, in the habit.

An example: People used to laugh at the way I spoke with my daughter when she was young. When Eva was just one, I took her to a dinner with my grad school research group. I set her up in a high chair and asked if she wanted her crayons and mat. I heard gentle titters from my colleagues but said nothing.

I got her set up with some things to occupy her. She started banging them around. It was happy noise but also disruptive, given where we were. I let her know that didn't work at the restaurant table, and I asked her to stop. I treated her politely, using a fairly normal tone of voice, without babying what I was saying. My colleagues thought it was hilarious. One even asked, "Why are you asking her that?"

The thing was—Eva stopped. And so did my colleagues' laughter. I responded that I talked to her like that because she understood what I was saying and was very able to act on it.

Babies *can* control themselves—just not for very long. They can make themselves stop, but that's about it. At that point, the parent or caregiver needs to change the environment so the baby isn't required to *stay* stopped.

Watching parents in a coffee shop repeatedly tell a two-year-old to stop touching the display unit is frustrating. Every time the parent says stop, the child stops. Wonderful! Invariably the parent turns away, though, and what's the kid left to do? So they start touching it again. It's right there, literally at the kid's eye level. Consider this when you're standing in line at a coffeeshop or grocery store: the things at *your knee level* are enticingly present right in the *face for small children*. Most parents offer nothing else to occupy the child—no objects, no strategies, no attention. So of course the little one is going to go back to it again and again. Why would we expect anything different?

It's all about setting good limits. We need to stop kids *before* they're chewing on someone's shoe! So how do you know what a good limit is for this kid, on this activity, under these conditions?

Limits necessarily change with age. You intuitively know you wouldn't give the same limit to a one-year-old, a three-year-old, and a seven-year-old. You already know you wouldn't give the same limit for playing with food and pushing a sibling. And you wouldn't give the same limit to throwing a ball in your own house versus in a store with lots of plate glass windows.

Kids often want to do things that don't work well for the people around them, but clamping down on them doesn't serve them well. Look for ways to set limits on kids' behavior that redirects their energy in more acceptable ways. Jumping on the couch? It needs to stop, but jumping on the floor or outside might be fine. I heard this limit from a mom who knows her four boys very well: "No jumping on the couch. Or *off* the couch!"

How do you know you're setting a good limit? Ask yourself:

1. Are people safe?

2. Are people (the child *and* others) being respected?

3. Are other people's things being respected?

4. Will it help the child learn what is good, responsible, and respectful?

The next section, "Following Through," offers examples and a set of steps to use for setting and maintaining good limits.

Things to Try

1. Look for the next time you want a child to stop or change what they're doing. Be clear within yourself about what the issue is for you before you speak to the child. Notice if you're angry or frustrated before you speak.

2. The next time you're setting a limit for a child, do a mental check. Are all the people involved, including the child, being respected by this limit and the way it's being set? If not, adjust the limit or the way you're talking.

3. When you're setting a limit, think about how you can use it to help the child learn what's behind it—not just the desired behavior (e.g., not jumping on the couch), but the bigger picture behind it.

Following Through

One very important thing to keep in mind about limits is that they only work if you actually follow through. I hear a lot of parents give in to their kids, and it's not doing anyone any good. It starts out as "no." Then it gets more emphatic, then louder, and eventually turns into a "yes" when the child pesters long enough. And how long is long enough? Well, that's right up until the "yes," of course!

It's important to ask what kids are learning when we set limits. *And* what they're learning when we let those limits evaporate.

A big part of children's cognitive development falls under what's called *social cognition*. That's all the understanding they build about other people, themselves, the internal workings of the mind, and the way social groups work. Through the limits we set and how we follow through on them, children come to understand us—how we work, what makes us tick, and what makes us ticked off. When I suggest we ask, "What am I teaching in this moment?," it largely points to children's developing social cognition: they are learning about themselves, us as parents/teachers, and our values.

Limits also help children build their understanding of causation, as they learn to connect their actions with the consequences. So we set limits. And *only* the ones we're OK actually following through on.

Maybe you've heard something like this (or even said it—I know I have): "If you don't clean those up, I'm throwing them away!" The problem is: are you really? If not, the limit is worse than useless. It doesn't establish the actual zone of desired behavior, and furthermore it teaches the child that what you say is empty.

If you're at the park and the child is acting up and won't work with you and won't stop, saying this isn't going to help them: "If you do that one more time, we're leaving!" All righty— then there's that one more time. Now you're stuck. If you don't want to have to leave, you're in a pickle. The good news is, it's actually OK to back out of a bad limit.

Let's go back to the one I'm guilty of: threatening to throw toys out that aren't put away. I'm not really able to bring myself to do that, and that makes it a problem to say it in the first place. The threat comes out in frustration (and yes, it has, more than once), and it isn't one I can actually follow through with. Having realized that the last time it happened, I was very up front with the kids. I acknowledged that I had set a limit I wasn't actually OK with—*and* that that wasn't helpful. I said why I was so frustrated. And I asked them to problem solve with me so that we could a) make the house more comfortable for me and others and b) come up with a plan for maintaining that. They were happy to do that. Much happier, I might add, than they'd been just a few minutes prior with a mom who was blowing her top and setting unreasonable, unrealistic limits.

Limits keep things clear. And all children, especially young children, want clarity. It feels safer. Rather than being merely constraining, limits are actually a kind of safety net for kids— which is why all kids should get them.

Unlike consequences, limits don't have to be set up in advance. It would be impractical to think that parents could anticipate every infraction a kid could think up. Kids are far too inventive for that! Instead, **good limits are responsive to the situation, to health and safety, and to the needs of others.**

Here are some examples:

Your toddler is banging a cup on the table. Delighted by the loud noise and ringing sounds, they squeal and laugh and do it over and over again. That's really cute. Unless you're the folks at the table two-and-a-half feet away. What your child is doing should not impose on others around you.

Here's how to set the limit: Take the cup away gently, and explain, "That noise is too loud for the café where we are. It's really fun to make, but it doesn't work here. It's not nice for the other people sitting near us. Let's try that again when we get home." Then return the cup. If the child goes to bang it again, reinforce the limit. If the child can't refrain from doing it again, you keep the cup.

A preschooler is unable to share and wrenches the toys back anytime another child (sibling, classmate) tries to use them. It's causing arguments and looks as if it could get physical.

Here's how to set the limit: Go to the child and offer support. "I see you're having trouble sharing these. It's nice to be able to have them all to yourself, but our toys are for everyone to use. So we need to find a way for you to have some and for others to be able to use them too. How could we do that?" Ideas include setting a time limit, such as two minutes, divide the toys, play together, or work out some other kind of plan/agreement with the child. "OK, so [repeat the agreement]." Then leave the child to play—and stay close. If they repeat the behavior, return promptly and reinforce the limit. If the child can't stop the behavior, transition them to a different activity, firmly yet kindly, reassuring them that they can try this one again later (and specify a time—that same day or tomorrow).

A child in the classroom is seeking attention by goofing off to get laughs. They're not focused on their work, and they're disrupting classmates. Children should not meet their own needs in ways that undermine themselves and others.

<u>Here's how to set the limit:</u> Go over to the student and check in privately. "It looks like you're having trouble getting started. It's pretty funny making that noise, but that's not OK in the classroom. Your classmates need this time to work, and so do you. Let's take a look at this writing and figure out what you need." Then leave the child to work. If they repeat the behavior, return and reinforce the limit. If the child can't refrain at this point, move them to a different seat in the classroom.

Do you see the trend? There are several steps to the process of setting and maintaining a limit:

1. Approach the child—proximity is essential. Don't try yelling or correcting from across the room.

2. Name the issue—give the child the language for understanding what you are not OK with.

3. Acknowledge the interest or need the child is meeting— show that you see where they are coming from and empathize.

4. Explain why that behavior doesn't work.

5. Name the desired behavior—give the child the language for understanding what you want.

6. Leave—give the child room and time to regulate.

7. Return if the behavior continues and repeat the limit exactly as it was stated—it reinforces the meaning of the words and your authority to set limits.

8. Return if it still continues and change the situation or move the child.

The key here is consistency, not flawless perfection. Children adapt very quickly to our expectations. They're masterful at knowing who means what they say and who is a pushover. Be like my friend Karla, who calmly shut down her boys clamoring for candy with a simple, "When was the last time you heard me change a no to a yes?"

Things to Try

1. For one day (or even a week), each time you need to set a limit, try thinking of one additional way you could solve the same issue.

2. When following through on a limit that isn't holding (step 7), check to see how you sound. If it's frustrated or angry, take a breath and adjust. Be careful to restate the limit just as you said it before, without extra words or threats.

3. If the limit doesn't hold (step 8), make whatever changes you need to as calmly as you can. Staying calm helps you, the child, and also your success with your next limit setting.

Explaining Why

When my nephew Chad was ten years old, in the midst of my stopping him from doing something he wanted to, he surprised me by saying, "I like that you explain why I can't."

Let's look closer at #4 from the list above: *4. Explain why that behavior doesn't work.* Why is explaining the reason behind the limit so important?

I'll start with a story. Writing this book has been a lot of fun, in part because people keep sharing all kinds of stories with me. A couple of months into writing, I told a friend about the topic for this book and she spontaneously shared this story, which perfectly illustrates how explaining shapes kids' thinking!

When Sharon's daughter Kim was younger, she went away with school to science camp. (It's a big thing here in the science-loving San Francisco Bay Area. At many schools 5th graders take a multi-day sleep-away field trip focused on science.) Sharon had gone along as one of the parent chaperones. Often, several schools attend at the same time, which gives kids a glimpse of life beyond their familiar range of home and school. Kim and her classmates noticed immediately that the kids from the other school were hard to deal with. These other kids were running around all over, making a lot of noise, slamming doors. They were disrespectful to the staff and messy in the shared spaces—basically, not your top pick for travel companions.

When Kim complained to her mom about them, Sharon observed, "Well, yeah. This is why we always explain to you. You understand why not to. We don't slam doors because it's disrespectful to other people's property, because it is disruptive to other people, and because it's not safe for you. Their parents have only told them not to. And now that they're someplace where their parents can't see them, they're having at it."

As Sharon's story shows, explaining the rationale behind our rules is the piece that will help kids deeply internalize that behavior. Yes, it is possible to instill the fear of God (or whomever) into kids and make them behave. But will they, when you're not there? Parents, teachers, and mental health counselors around the country will tell you: the answer is no.

We need to set limits because we need kids to be safe and respectful and responsible. We need to *explain* those limits so kids can internalize what's being asked of them. Explaining kicks it up a notch, so kids can go from just compliance to buying in.

When to Start

We can fairly easily agree that explaining things leads to deeper understanding. But when do you start? Can young children really understand the reasons behind why we want them to do something? What do kids get when we use "why" or "because" to justify our limits?

· Kids are more capable on this score than you might think.

You know that kids understand if they can respond appropriately. An even stronger indication that they understand is if they start using the behavior themselves. In a 2004 study published in the journal *Language and Education*, researchers Donna McWilliam and Christine Howe showed that as little as ten minutes a day for four days did wonders for four-year-olds. After four-days of instruction from a researcher, the preschoolers were using more explanations with their classmates—both in terms of asking other children to explain why and in justifying their own claims when challenged. Four days. Ten minutes a day. That's all it took to shift the way these little kids expressed their thinking in interactions with other kids. Pretty impressive.

So when it comes to offering kids a reason for why we need them to do something, there is no doubt that we can bump it up a notch—starting very young.

Here's an example of what it can look like with an older child. I bumped into a friend at the yoga studio/tea house I like to go to. As we stood chatting, she mentioned that she had just come from a parenting class she has taken over the past few years. She finds that it's helped her navigate the changing needs of parenting as her three children have grown from being little kids into teenagers.

The topic fell to bedtime, and I shared a bit about sleep needs in childhood and adolescence, and about how common teen sleep shortage is. She had a lot of questions, so we started talking about children's biological needs and how to manage kids' sleep in today's tech-enabled, high-pressure environment.

My friend Tina asked about my family's 10:00 p.m. bedtime for our teens: "Is that hard?"

I laughed out loud and told her quite honestly, "No. And yes."

Setting a bedtime that's earlier than many other families is something I started when our kids were very young. So in some ways it's not hard because they have lived with it for a long time and they know to expect it. But in other ways it's very hard. In real life, sticking to it is something that frequently needs to be renegotiated—tucked back in from time to time—because it slips, or their needs change and we have to update the norm.

Tina was having trouble because her youngest child was bucking his bedtime. At twelve, he's very aware that he is not yet a teenager. He's fighting that the rest of the family get to stay up.

Here's the advice I offered Tina. At a quiet time one afternoon, open a conversation with your son about bedtime. Acknowledge that he wishes it were different—let him hear that you see how he feels. Explain the reason for the rule—remind him that he's *not* as big as the others. He's not as old, not as tall, and his body and brain need the extra sleep while he's growing.

Reinforce what you expect—say it again. In fact, as children get older, *have them say it*. Think *internalization*. Actually saying the words, and hearing themselves say the words, shifts the regulation from you to them. It's a very helpful step in their process of internalizing what you want from them. Of course, their being willing to do it is another matter altogether...

One caveat about children. It's perfectly possible for your children to understand your explanation and refuse to go along with you. That's what it means to set a limit! As the parent (or caregiver) you're still responsible for them.

When to Do All That Explaining

Timing is important here. All of this needs to be done at some time *other than* bedtime or whenever the limit is being enforced. Limit setting and explanations are the context for what is needed. They need to be spelled out in advance, so that at bedtime, it's clear what's required. It just needs to happen. If there's pushback, there needs to be a pre-established set of consequences. Those, too, need to be worked out in advance so that there's no need for discussion at the height of the conflict.

Having all this worked out before the conflict helps you stay calmer. That's critical because once you're worked up, 1) you're not thinking as clearly, and 2) you're letting the child gain ground that is not theirs to have.

Obviously, it's easier said than done. It can be hard work to corral kids at the end of the day. If parents work, and kids' days are full, by the end of the day everyone is feeling a bit shot and overdone. That makes it harder, and thus even more important, to stick to what's needed.

Every child is an individualized case. Some children can hear the explanation at the time of the limit setting, and others practically go ballistic when you limit them. As a parent, or teacher, or anyone working with kids, you have to learn whom you're working with. The ideas in this book will help you, but you still have to tailor them to the child who is in front of you.

What Makes for a Good Explanation?

In general, kids are good at following our line of thinking. One thing you can do is help the child connect what you're saying to things they already know. It's clear that both our understanding and our memory are improved when we connect new ideas to older ones. That's the process of elaboration I discussed in Chapter 5, in the section on "Compliance or Resistance."

Research on this topic is strong, especially in classroom settings. Kids learn more when they are guided to connect new ideas to their prior knowledge. (If you're interested in this, British researcher Neil Mercer has studied patterns of classroom talk for three decades, connecting how children talk to how they think. His 1999 paper with Rupert Wegerif and Lyn Dawes on the development of reasoning is a good example here.) The good news is it's actually fairly easy to teach kids new patterns of language use, at home or school—and explaining leads to deeper understanding.

So when you're explaining to a child your reasons for a particular limit, you can tap into their prior experience and understanding. Remind them of things that have happened in the past. Ask them to make those connections themselves.

Things to Try

1. Limits go beyond saying no to saying what you *do* want, and why. Take a moment to be clear in your own mind why you want the child to behave the way you're asking them to. Just to stop isn't enough. Ask why—how does the child's behavior conflict with your values?

2. When a child is not doing what you want, try to see whether it is willful disobedience or more that the child is very focused on what they want to do. When children are really occupied with what they're doing, you have to break through to get them thinking. Explaining why you want what you're asking for can help here.

3. Recruit children's willingness to work with you. Explanations take a moment to give, but they appeal to kids' sense of fairness.

Stop Means Stop

Stop means stop. The first time.

Have you ever had a little kid tug on you repeatedly? Or bump into the table you're writing on? Whine in the grocery store? Have you ever had an older brother wrestle you and hold you under water? Did it stop when you wanted it to?

"Stop means stop" is first and foremost about safety. And it works both ways. When I say stop, the kids need to. Right then. And when *they* say stop, I need to, too. Really.

Here's why it's a safety thing. If I yell *Stop!* to a kid running toward the street, I need to know that's going to halt them in their tracks. If someone is pushing me, I need to know that when I tell them to stop, they will cease annoying me. If I'm doing something one of the kids really doesn't like, they need to know that it's in their power to make things OK for themselves.

I established "stop means stop" when my firstborn was very small. She got it instantly, as did her brother when he came along. Our kids know that they can exert their needs and that their dad and I will listen. It's almost sacrosanct in our house because it says to the children that they can keep themselves safe.

This is important for children because they have so little control over their lives—they should at least be allowed to say what happens to their bodies in a play-like situation.

One of the most uncomfortable parenting moments I've ever witnessed involved a dad "playing" with his young son. He was a friend's husband, and a pretty hands-off dad. During a party, he started a tickle fight with his three-year-old son, Martin.

It was bad from the beginning. The little guy was playing on the floor when his dad came up from behind, scooped him up and started forcefully tickling him. Martin wailed no, but Dad kept going. He kept saying he was just tickling him and that Martin should play along. Martin continued to protest, getting increasingly upset. Unbelievably, the dad just kept going, tossing him in the air as he "tickled" him. By the time the boy was crying, the dad was laughing about what a little baby he was being. Looking around me, I realized no else seemed to notice.

I agonized at the time whether to intervene for Martin. I got caught by all the social niceties—I was a guest; no one likes his parenting criticized—and settled for playing with the boy once his dad set him down, helping him get settled and calmer. I felt awful—both for what I had witnessed and for my own inaction.

Do you find yourself wondering if I was making too big a deal of this? The dad just wanted to play, right?

Let's take a look at playing. For starters—**in playing, both sides are meant to have fun.** If they aren't, by definition, then it's not playing. It may be *intended* as play, but what's happening is something else altogether.

The dad in this story scooped up his son with no warning or invitation. He typically had little interaction with his son, so he wasn't likely to know what his son enjoyed. He didn't notice his son was happily engaged in what he was doing. When his son protested, the father rebuked him. This little boy was not enjoying having his father pull and tug at him. All he had in his arsenal was "Stop!" And that didn't work. When his dad blew right through it, the kid resorted to yelling and crying. When his dad finally did stop, more out of disinterest than consideration, in the end he castigated a three-year-old for not playing along.

Does this sound like any of the current discussions about rape culture? It's not as far removed as you might think.

If children grow up hearing that "stop means stop" they internalize the belief that they have:

1. A right to determine how their body is treated.

2. The responsibility to allow other people that same right.

Even if the children you interact with are still young, try to imagine how being able to say "stop" could play out in a dating relationship when they're older. Obviously, words alone are not sufficient. They don't tell a child what to do when someone refuses to stop; that skill has to be built as well. But words instill the necessary precursor to making someone stop—the belief that you have the right to control what happens to you.

This one simple statement can have huge ripple effects on what children think and how they act on it later. It's protective for kids and teens, all the way from grade school through college. From bullying to girl drama to romantic relationships, growing up with the belief that *stop means stop* helps kids establish and maintain healthy boundaries—healthy because children know they can set them and that they have to respect other people's.

Things to Try

1. Try talking to your family or classroom about this idea. What do they think?

2. If it's important to you that *stop means stop*, start implementing it by noticing when it doesn't happen.

3. Bringing others on board can be difficult. If you see a *stop* not being listened to, really stop everyone in the moment to say what you just observed, and that it's important to you that people know they will be heard when they say stop.

"After"

This small word is one the most powerful in the English language. It puts the power for children to do what they want to in their own hands.

I started showing my students the Marshmallow Test video in about 2009. Someone at Stanford had redone the study, and the video summary on YouTube was short and visually appealing. It also had a great soundtrack—key for classroom use!

As I described earlier, in the original Marshmallow study, Walter Mischel devised a simple test of kids' willpower. Four-year-olds were brought into a room and offered a marshmallow by a researcher. Wonderful! Then they were told that if they waited until the researcher came back, they could have two marshmallows. Now, every child in the study wanted two treats. But not all the children were able to make themselves wait. And therein lay the meat of the study.

Mischel says he never intended the study as a test. He was more interested in examining kids' *strategies* for self-regulating. Later, he became fascinated with the life outcomes associated with either waiting or not. His excellent book *The Marshmallow Test* (2014) discusses the follow-up study done forty years after. Throughout the book, he stresses that while waiting *is* associated with better life outcomes, **strategies for waiting can be learned.**

Here is the power of "after." *After* **is a simple tool to help children develop the ability to wait.** Most of them (just like many of us) aren't able to help themselves wait. It's hard work. It takes self-discipline. Children need support and structure from adults. "After" creates a clear linear structure in which the actions are transparent and the desired outcome is in sight. It communicates the value of doing what *needs* to be done first. And it does it in a simple, respectful way.

Imagine this scenario: a child wants to watch a video, and you're trying to get dinner together. You know they're hard to pull away from the screen; it causes arguments and makes dinner less pleasant. Watching after the meal alleviates all those battles. So you say, *"Yes, you can watch that. After dinner."*

Or this one: piles of laundry—*clean* laundry that you have taken the time and effort to wash—are piled up waiting to be folded and put away. Your teen wants to go see a friend. *"Yes, you can go over to Ryan's—after you finish folding the laundry."*

It works in the classroom or restaurant just as easily. Teachers, waitstaff, and anyone who encounters children in their work needs to have "after" in their back pocket, ready to pull out at any moment.

"It's fine to draw, after you finish your writing assignment."

"Yes, you can have some crayons, after you have been seated."

After offers kids a clear-cut path. It's a form of conditional reasoning: this, then that. For young children, this is especially important since their sense of time is not fully developed. It's much clearer for children under five to know that something they want will happen after an event or activity than to tell them to wait a certain number of minutes. For older children and teens, "after" sets clear boundaries between what is expected of them and their actions.

There's another great thing about using "after." At the same time that the adult offers structural support for the child's self-regulation, the adult also gets out of the way. The child is now responsible—in charge, if you will—of whether or not what they want actually happens. They can have it as long as the other *needed* thing happens first. And in many cases, *when* they get what they want is also up to them—you can take ten minutes to fold laundry or sixty. The end result is the same to the grown-up, yet there's a built-in motivation to work more quickly if what awaits you is of value to you. And even if you do work slowly this time, that creates the opportunity to reflect on the idea that you might want to go faster next time.

The beautiful thing about "after" is that it helps kids practice self-restraint, with the bonus that if what the child wants doesn't happen, it's not your fault! It won't work instantaneously, of course. Stick with it though, and be consistent, and it will work.

Things to Try

1. Waiting in line is hard for very young children. The next time you're stuck waiting, turn it into a game of "after." Talk to the child about what you could do after you've finished this errand. It doesn't even have to be real things—making it fantastical can be fun to kids. What you want to reinforce is the idea that this thing is going to happen first, and then get them to put their attention on when it's finished.

2. When you need to tell a child they can't do something because other things need to get done, try to find a way to say, "Yes, after . . ."

3. If you're with a child who's having a hard time waiting their turn, acknowledge how hard it can be to wait. Then get them thinking about how much fun they will have when it's their turn. For example, "It's hard to wait for the swing, isn't it. How high do you want to go today?"

"It's Not on the List"

When my children were very little we 'enjoyed' the same grocery store trials and tribulations as most families: "Can I have...?" "I want these!" "Let's get..." followed by yelling, complaining, whining, and crying. Stores are intentionally arranged and designed to create desire. In case you're not aware of this, literally millions of dollars are spent in marketing research to figure out what shelf to place food on and how to arrange those annoying stacks that stick out into the aisles—all to promote more sales. Especially last-minute sales.

We had some premium-grade meltdowns (theirs, not mine—though there were times I was tempted . . .). I've walked out of the store leaving a full cart behind me, calling out over my shoulder to the store manager that I hoped to be back in a few minutes, and if not, well, I was sorry. I realized very quickly that I couldn't take several years of this. It was starting to look as if the only solution was to do all my shopping by myself—a logistical nightmare, given my work and caregiving schedule.

I invented a rule, which we went over before leaving the house each time we went shopping: **"If it's not on the list, it doesn't go in the cart."**

To be honest, this had a couple of downsides for me. It meant I actually had to take the time to write out a list anytime I went to get groceries or household things. It also meant I had to hold myself to the same standard (which I did, even before my kids could read). No more spontaneous chip purchases. No more grabbing those cookies that looked so tasty. Hard to stick to!

The upside to the rule was life altering though, and I heartily recommend you try it. Any time the kids started to ask for some kind of treat or junk food, I could simply say: "It's not on the list, so we aren't buying it today." It took several times, of course, for the idea to fully sink in. I had to be 100 percent consistent. As I said in Chapter 7's section "The Easy Way," kids are like velociraptors testing the fence. Let it slip one once and they have incentive to keep testing to find the next slip in their favor.

Over time, my children almost never asked for treats in a store. When they did, I simply reminded them politely, "It isn't on the list," and they accepted it. That may seem unbelievable, but the kids knew I would follow through. My sister Lisa reminded me of a story showing how fully my kids internalized the rule. When my son Oscar was very little, my sister came to visit. We were all in the store, and Oscar's eyes lit up when he saw a box of donuts. Lisa asked if he wanted them. He answered with a huge sigh, saying, "I do want them, but they're not on Mama's list." Good aunt that she is, Lisa asked if *she* could buy them, and made for one very happy nephew.

This is one of the many benefits of using clear limits, consistent follow-through, and explaining your rationale to your kids: they start to listen to you. I could sail through a store with no whining. If you have kids, you know how great that is!

What developed in place of whining or yelling was a clever "Could we put it on the list next time?" which I found pretty amusing. I tackled that by saying we would discuss it at home.

The other thing that developed was my children's ability to independently ask for food they wanted, when we were still at home. They could choose the appropriate time—when the list was being generated.

This was fantastic, and I have to say, unexpected. First of all, remembering to talk to me about something they wanted in the future took both planning and patience—terrific qualities for young children to practice. It was also fantastic because it gave us the opportunity to *talk* about what they wanted and how that fit into our family's values for food health and our budget concerns. Bringing it up at the house meant we could take the time to discuss it outside of the frenzy of the store and needing to get through the task. **"It's not on the list" created a conversation, rather than a fight.** And it saved us money to boot.

I know it works. And not just for me. Out grocery shopping with my seventeen-year-old daughter, I overheard a mom and her children in line. You know all those last-minute treats for you to succumb to while you wait? Market research shows that our willpower is weakest when we're almost done and waiting to get out. That's *why* all those goodies are there in line to tempt us.

Well, it was working. I had already seen these three kids in the store, and they were really well behaved. They had been helping their mom throughout the store, and they were polite and playful with each other. Really model behavior. And then, while in the line, the littlest one picked up some candy and turned to her mom. I was delighted to hear a simple, polite "It's not on the list" from the mother. And down went the candy, no complaint, no fuss. No issue. Because this mom obviously levels with her kids. She also follows through.

"It's not on the list" can work for you too.

Things to Try
1. Talk to your kids about how you want a grocery store run to go.
2. Ask the kids in your life how they feel when someone keeps pestering them to do something they've already said no to.
3. Try implementing "If it's not on the list, it doesn't go in the cart."

"If I'm on the Phone, the Answer Is No"

Here's one more example of a simple and effective limit. If you spend time with young kids, you know they want you when they want you. That never seems truer than when you're in the middle of something. For me, this was phone calls. When my kids were little, as soon as I was on the phone, they were at my heels asking for things. Since I was distracted and wanted to get back to what I was doing, I usually gave an unwilling OK or at best a noncommittal "mmhmm."

I was creating a monster. (Or two.) Not surprisingly, this was working pretty well for my kids. It kept up and intensified, to the point that I was snapping at them and losing my cool. I needed a way to get control back for how and when they were asking. And I needed to set a boundary for myself so that my phone calls weren't always interrupted. **I set a new rule: "If I'm on the phone, the answer is no."**

As with "It's not on the list" it took *several* times to really set in. My follow-through was key—if I got off the call to find they had done/taken/started whatever it was anyway, I had to intervene. Over time, they accepted that to ask for something while I was on the phone was futile.

And then they got clever again. "Do I have to not play on the computer?" "Can I not have a cookie?" If they could force the no, they could happily do whatever they wanted! Such power!

It was great watching them experiment with language, with me, and with their social understanding to see if they could work around me. (I didn't fall for it, of course.)

Also like "It's not on the list," this new rule opened up conversations—once I was off the phone and not in the thick of things. We could talk about how and when to ask for what they wanted. I explained why I needed not to be interrupted. I wanted them to know I was available if they truly needed me, and that they wouldn't die if they had to wait a few minutes. We set an agreement: no interruptions unless there was blood. (And yes, that happened too—you can end a phone call really quickly if you need to!)

This might strike you as just behavior management. I'd like to point to more. For me **this is about what kids understand.**

Kids need explanations because it helps them build their world view. (Bonus: it also builds their vocabulary!) Children want to work with you—they truly do. Even while they also want their own way and the things that are of interest to them. Underneath it all is a more pressing desire to be connected to you. That's why children need to understand what you will allow, and why. And *within that,* they also need opportunities to flex their thinking and seek to meet their own interests.

The trick is that our words help them get there. Remember to ask yourself, What am I teaching in this moment? You're teaching three things:

1. *Who I am.* Setting these kinds of rules makes clear what we expect from kids. Using the rules consistently teaches them that our words are our bond—we mean what we say, and we will follow through. A clear structure is like a safety net for children. It builds their sense of trust in us.

2. *What the world is like.* Setting and applying these kinds of rules also helps kids build a solid understanding of the world, especially the people in it—who they are and how they work. Kids' social cognition is developing regardless of how we talk to them. Beginning at birth, babies observe other people and slowly map out their intentions. They *will* figure out the people in their lives and what motivates them. The key is that how we speak to

kids can create a sense that the world is fair and trustworthy—or the opposite. Optimally, our words can teach kids that people have power and that they need to use it responsibly.

3. *Self-regulation.* These clear-cut rules also help children build their own ability to regulate themselves—to wait, to ask, to get creative. It's not OK to yell and whine every time you want something. But not yelling and whining takes effort. Little kids (and bigger ones too) need our support. When we go beyond our own yelling, or just saying no incessantly, we create for kids the opportunity to build these skills. Their abilities may surprise you.

Things to Try

1. When the child you are with starts whining or vying for something, stop what you're doing and clearly reset. Tell them that whining isn't going to work and let them know you'd be happy to talk to them about it another time. Then move on. If the whining continues, remind them *one time* of what you've said and then ignore it. If it's an option, consider leaving where you are and trying another time.

2. Take a look at what drives you crazy—for me it was the gimme's in the store and pestering when I was on the phone. Find what it is for you. How could you organize it so that it goes better for you?

3. Slow down. (Yes, this is harder to do than say.) When we slow down, we can recall our better selves. Remember to ask yourself, What am I teaching in this moment? How could you shift so that what you're teaching is more in alignment with your goals for the child?

9

More Tools for the Toolkit

Say less, sing more

Like a runner in a long distance race, we're on the back side of the field headed for the finish line! So far we've looked at the basics of language development and taken a deeper look at the research. We've seen how to help kids learn from their mistakes, how our words can shift the control from us to them, and how a positive framing can help kids find more and better solutions. We've seen how questions can deepen kids' understanding and looked at how to set and maintain good limits that help kids manage themselves and their responsibilities.

There's still some more I want to show you.

Here I draw tools from practical experience more than research, including why it's a good idea to hold off on sarcasm with younger children, thoughts on teaching kids to be polite, how to shift our speech when we're worked up or frustrated, and what our use of pronouns is telling children.

No Sarcasm—Really

Kids are funny. They are capable and incapable all at the same time. This is as true of teens as it is very young children. It shows up early in language development, since their comprehension outstrips production for so long. Two-year-olds can barely say anything. Maybe they're speaking two- to three-word sentences, but it's often really hard to make out what they're saying. We don't tend to have deep conversations with a two-year-old.

Yet here's the surprising thing: Even very young children can understand all kinds of complex things we say. One place this shows up is with indirect speech acts. *Indirect speech act* is simply the term for implying what we mean without actually saying it. For example, a parent might ask, "Is the door closed?" Children as young as two-years old can understand that the parent isn't *actually* asking literally whether the door is closed or not, but for it *to be* closed. There's an implication behind the words. Toddlers understand and can interpret it. The average two-year-old knows the correct response to the question is to get up and close the door. (The average twelve-year-old knows this too, by the way; they just think it's funny to give a literal answer.)

That's a pretty sophisticated use of language. So if a two-year-old can read between the lines like this, why can't they understand sarcasm?

Sarcasm is tricky. There are several things going on simultaneously with sarcasm, and they conflict. Young children can be genuinely confused by this. When you talk to a child, they perceive and interpret the input on multiple channels:

- The words you say
- The tone you use
- The expression on your face
- The energy coming off you

With sarcasm, these channels don't line up. It does, of course, matter what prompts the sarcasm. If it's just humor, that's slightly easier. But if it's frustration or anger, it can feel like a minefield to a younger child. Your words say one thing, your tone says something different, the expression doesn't fit, and the energy coming off you is definitely funky.

Take the example of a young child being asked to clean up. As they carry their plate, food drops to the floor. The parent gibes, "Nice job." The child can see food on the floor, so they can assume there's a problem, but the parent is saying it's OK. Then again, it doesn't look like they mean it. But they're saying it, so do they mean it? Confusing. For kids who are particularly adept at reading a parent's social cues, this can even be highly distressing.

Not sure if kids can actually read your energy? Do you know the phrase "laugh and the whole world laughs with you"? Ever caught someone else's yawn? Humans as a species are *very* good at reading emotional energy. And children even more so.

There's also the chance kids will breeze through the whole thing and not notice the conflicting input. They'll believe they really did do a good job—not what you want them to think!

When Does Sarcasm Work?

Fourth grade marks a new level of understanding for kids. At this point, age nine or ten, something just clicks, and most of them simply *get* sarcasm. They think they've discovered it and that it's hilarious. Their reading interests typically turn darker here— think Lemony Snickett's *A Series of Unfortunate Events*. Terribly funny stuff to the average fourth grader.

If that seems surprisingly late to you, consider this: even fourth grade may be too soon for some kids. A teacher I know who taught fourth and fifth grades for years is now teaching sixth grade, and has found that she can be her goofy, sarcastic self and the kids *all* get it! Jessica told me, "At fourth, half the class got it, and the others didn't. They just thought I was weird. And not in a good way! Or they realized that the others got it and they didn't, and they couldn't figure out what they had missed. It was upsetting to them to be left out."

Personally, I couldn't wait for my kids to finally get sarcasm. I have a very dark sense of humor, and I leashed it for my kids' early years. I recall vividly the day my ten-year-old asked why his sister got the bigger piece of pie. I looked him dead in the eye and totally straight face said "Because I love her more." He was shocked! And then he looked at me again and saw my eyes laughing. My son laughed so hard he practically fell over!

Families That Are Highly Sarcastic

Some families enjoy a highly sarcastic sense of humor. In my experience, children in these families do learn to interpret—and use—sarcasm at a younger age. I'm neutral on whether that's a good thing or not. But it is consistent with the main point of this book: kids are wired to learn what they hear.

Things to Try

1. With a younger child, try saying something you don't mean and play with your tone of delivery. If you're straight-faced, what do they do? What if you use a mocking tone? If you take a playful tone, is it any different?

2. With a child nine years or older, try saying something outrageous as if you believe it and see how they react!

3. With a teen, try a total deadpan delivery to catch them up. Just stay away from topics you know are truly important to them.

Manners

I grew up in the South, in the land of "please" and "thank you," of "yes, ma'am" and "no, sir." I still use them, though I've let *sir* and *ma'am* drop, living out West. Anytime we travel home, though, I have to coach my poor little California kids on how important it is for them to use *sir* and *ma'am* while in Georgia.

Despite the ubiquity of these words, I'd never thought to ask myself, Why do we want kids to say please and thank you? Why do we say it ourselves? Where did this form of politeness come from?

On her *Brain Pickings* blog, Maria Popova offers an explanation from David Graeber's book *Debt: The First 5,000 Years*. According to Graeber, the custom of saying *please* and *thank you* started in the sixteen and seventeenth centuries out of economic, commercial revolution. Graeber is an anthropologist at the London School of Economics, so he's a reputable voice on such matters. His research points to the habit of *please* and *thank you* deriving from the leveling of the playing field in society, which came as the commercial class broke free from feudalism. The idea arose at that time that even "common" people were deserving of the same treatment and deference that had previously only been accorded to the feudal lords. History is interesting stuff!

I wasn't familiar with this history. Reading it though, it immediately made sense why kids rebel at being told to "say please." Or perhaps worse, being prompted in a sing-song voice, "What's the magic word?" Many people in US society believe that saying please and thank you are signs of moral upbringing. I certainly do. Children are taught to parrot these niceties and scolded when they don't. Yet adults often aren't very polite when we speak to children. Adults often command children pretty baldly: "Pick those up." "Stop that!" "Don't hit your sister."

The rule for these manners, then, seems to be this: they are for children to use and learn, but adults get to play by a different set. It makes sense to me that kids find it anywhere from frustrating to humiliating when they're made to say things like "please."

Children feel this power divide keenly. They know very early on that that they cannot speak to adults the same way adults speak to them. And let me be crystal clear here: I'm not saying kids *are* on the same playing field as adults. It would be a mistake to think that and a mistake to treat them that way. I'm saying it's worth looking at what our words are actually teaching children to think.

When I need my kids to do something, I make that clear. It's not a request. I'm not asking them if they want to or if they would please do it. There's no opening for their opinion or for them to say, "No, I don't want to." I'm stating what needs to happen. Yet I also find that being polite can be part of the communication. It's not hard for me to say, "Pick up your blocks now, please."

Likewise, when they've completed things they need to do or are expected to take care of, I think it's fine to acknowledge that effort: "Thank you for clearing your dishes." I do appreciate their contributions to the running of the household. I don't thank them for everything, but I do say thank you often. My kids know that their contributions matter.

I was told by elementary school teachers a long time ago that they have observed that the children who say "please" and "thank you" the most are the ones whose *parents* say them the most. In the intervening years, I've heard this same thing from many other educators—even from an etiquette specialist! We know in child development that children learn more from our modeling than from our instructions. It's not just what we say to them, it's how we say it.

If it's important to you that children in your classroom or in your care learn to be polite, know that kids learn manners better from us when we model them than when we instruct. Yet they also need our instruction, so the trick is to model politeness even when we're teaching.

In my child development class I showed a video clip that gives an overview of what development looks like from birth to age two. The last part has the sweetest scene of preschoolers enjoying make-believe tea at their pint-sized table. Their teacher is folded up into a small chair with them, "pouring" the tea. One little guy pipes up, "More tea!" (I love pointing out to my students that young children can be so delighted asking for more of nothing!)

The teacher asks him very conversationally, "What do you need to ask?" The little guy cheerfully belts out, "Please!"

Luckily, she doesn't give in at this point. Instead, the teacher pushes for the complete thought, rather than the knee-jerk reaction. Just as conversationally as before, she asks him, "How do you say the whole thing?"

He comes back just as cheerfully with, "More tea, please!" thrusting his cup up in the air for her to "fill up."

The teacher reinforces this by repeating his full request: "More tea, please. Here you go," as she pours it to the brim. The little guy relishes his "tea," belting out, "Yum!"

My deal with kids is simply to ignore them if they *demand* something. When I'm new to working with them—for example, when I'm working in a new classroom or caregiving for the first time—I tell children that I use "please" when asking for something and that I'd like them to as well. Then after that first prompt, I just act as if I haven't heard them until they actually use the word *please*.

Also, like the master teacher in the video clip, I don't respond if *all* I get is the *please*. All children can manage this if they know you expect it—even very young children barely learning to speak. Here's an easy rule of thumb for when you're with a young child. If the child is at least two years old, they can manage a two-word sentence. It might sound like "more please" or "tea peese." If the child is at least three years old, they can manage a three-word sentence like "more tea please" or "peese more tea."

I like to be spoken to in full sentences, and spoken to politely. Maybe you're different on this. If not, though, give it a try.

Things to Try

1. Listen to what other adults say when working with kids. Do they prompt for *please* and *thank you*? Do they use them?

2. When you're working with a young child who demands something, start by explaining that in your class (or play yard, house, etc.): "We say *please* when we want something." Then wait to see what the child does.

3. If the child has been told you like to use *please*, try ignoring demands, whines, etc. Wait them out. See what they do. They'll be testing you at the same time.

Say Less

Most of us have known times when our words, no matter how carefully chosen, have fallen on deaf ears. Sometimes, it's a matter of too much input. Kids are wired to listen, but sometimes that gets short circuited.

Sometimes telegraphic speech is far more useful than long-winded explanations—especially if you're frustrated or frazzled. A simple, straightforward, "Shoes. Backpack. Door." is enough to get a seven-year-old out of the house with the things they need.

Notice there's a difference here between barking the orders at the child—"Shoes! Backpack! Door!"—and just speaking in single words. Both are short, but being barked at doesn't feel so good to the kid on the receiving end—which makes it harder for them to comply. So yes, we have to keep ourselves under as even a keel as we can. We're human, and at times our annoyance is going to creep into our voice. Try to soften and just keep moving.

Keep in mind the question, What am I teaching in this moment? Are you teaching kindness along with that responsibility? Or are you shaming your child at the same time you're getting them to school on time? The tone of your voice conveys a lot of information to the child. Dropping down to the simplest terms in a clear, calm voice can be a very effective strategy.

Saying less gives kids the essential information without the cloud of too many words. When time is tight or there's a lot going on or tempers are flaring, switching to telegraphic speech clears the way for a child to hear the most important parts. This is as true in the classroom as it is at home.

Remember, when kids are upset, or deeply engaged, or rushed, they don't hear us as well as they usually do. Well, they can *hear* just fine. But they're not *processing* it as well as they usually do. Telegraphic speech helps kids in two ways:

1. It strips out all but the essential content and helps the child focus in on what we need them to do.

2. It gives less ground for our own bad feelings to attach to—whether we're frustrated, angry, snarky, or just fed up. We end up sounding less bad when we say less.

Things to Try

1. Practice taking a long-winded directive and breaking it down into three or four key words. Work on keeping your tone conversational rather than sharp.

2. With young children, inject playfulness when you speak this way. Use silly voices or clap the beat of the words.

3. With older kids or teens, be sure to use a neutral tone. Telegraphic speech needs to sound friendly rather than snippy.

Sing Them to Their Rooms

Another great strategy when you're really angry or frustrated is to sing! It really doesn't matter if it's on key or not. The point here is that it's almost impossible to be angry and sing at the same time. This works best with young children, but it can startle even older children. It's not that helpful with teens, unfortunately.

When my son was very little, he could really push my buttons. When he talked back to me, all my Southern upbringing came roaring to the surface; it infuriated me to have my kids sass me. I also knew I didn't want to project that fury. So I sang! As I tossed him over my shoulder, fireman-style, I would carry my son off to his room so that we could both cool off, singing. LOUDLY.

♪ ♪*"I really don't like that. When you try to hit me, it hurts."*
♪ ♪

♫*"I can't let you do that. I'm taking you to your room for you to cool off. You can come out when you're ready to talk to me."* ♫

I would deposit him gently into his room, close the door, and walk away. It was always a race to see which of us cooled down faster.

Singing helps you and it helps the child. *You* because when you sing loudly, you can redirect some of your excess energy; as a result, you're not as upset and you're better able to control your emotions. *The child* because when you sing, your mouth is open and closer to smiling. A singing parent is much less scary than a yelling one.

Of course, if you think you're a really *bad* singer, you can use singing the way my friend Patty does in her classrooms: when the kids aren't listening, she sings at the top of her lungs until they *stop* talking!

Things to Try

1. Try this on your own first. Think of a recent time you had to cart off a young child to their room. Grit your teeth and say whatever it was you said then. Now try singing it.

2. You know when your buttons are pushed. As you feel yourself heat up, switch to singing to convey what you need to say to the child.

3. The next time you find yourself frustrated, see if you can head off the difficult behavior by singing at the beginning.

We/You

I can't tell you how often I hear parents make comments like, "We have to do his homework tonight."

This is a clear bleed of boundaries, and an important one to catch when we are talking to kids. *We* do not have to do the homework. *He* has to. *We* are there to support, or guide, or get the heck out of the way. But not to do it.

I call this kind of speech *pronoun abuse*, and I try to flag it gently and directly any time I hear a friend (or even myself!) using it. It's an indication that the parent has gotten too emotionally identified with what the child is doing.

Early into writing this book, I shared my idea of pronoun abuse with my friend Dan. Over lunch, I had heard it creep into his stories about his son's athletic prowess. So when he offered to read some of my writing and give me feedback, I picked these pages. He later called me on my "evil but accurate listening"!

Dan did see himself using "we" when talking about his kids, mostly his son Tony. He reflected it had probably started when Tony began playing hockey—Dan's favorite sport. Dan relished Tony's successes "shredding" teams with better records. Neither of Dan's kids had excelled athletically and Dan told me he'd let go of the idea of having athletic kids. Then Tony found hockey, fell in love, and started crushing it.

In his feedback on the book, Dan told me all of this—how he'd seen his slip into using "we" around hockey and his decision to catch it and stop using it. He graciously told me my writing "has already helped" and offered me this story!

It's easy to see that pronoun abuse shows up in how we talk to and about our kids. The question is—what is this way of speaking teaching the child? Let's look at a few examples.

Homework and School Work in General

"We have a big project due soon."

What this says is that the child is not alone (possibly good) or able to be (definitely bad). What kids draw from this is an understanding that we don't have confidence in them to do it on their own. That's worth a pause, isn't it?

Our universal goal for kids is to help them be able to do more on their own. That means we need to recognize that a child's homework/projects/chores are *theirs* to do. If they truly can't complete them, then the adult in charge needs to step in to restructure the task or environment so that the child can achieve competence and mastery. But let's be clear; the adult should not be doing any of the actual work.

Kids are pretty smart; they know that grown-ups are more capable than they are, and that grown-ups tend to know more. So if the grown-up says they need help, well then, they do. That's not helping them build independence. And it's not helping them build the confidence that being independent requires.

Athletics

"We had a gymnastics meet this weekend."

Does this make it clearer? Ask yourself, who was it on the mat—the parent or the child? The parent may have driven to the meet. Definitely paid for the lessons. Sat on uncomfortable bleachers for four hours. The parent is clearly involved and invested in the child's gymnastics. But the parent did not compete. The *athlete* competed. The *athlete* is the one who had the meet. The family *went to* the meet. This isn't a simple slip of the tongue. Pronoun abuse shows where a parent is overinvolved emotionally. And as with Dan's story, this shows up often around children's athletics.

So what is pronoun abuse telling kids? That they are not solely achieving this. Is that what we want them to hear? What we want them to believe?

School's In podcast recently interviewed Julie Lythcott-Haims, author of *How to Raise an Adult*. She listed the three signals that someone is overparenting: her first indicator was the use of *we*. Her example was also sports, noting that "*we* are not on the travel soccer team." She suggested the parent run a few laps on the field and then tell her who it is who is on the team.

College Applications

"We're applying to colleges this year."

This one is incredibly common for parents of teens, and it shows how complicated this is. Clearly, teens need their parents' assistance applying to college, a high stakes and complex task. Applications involve managing an incredible array of tasks and information, plus time management. One of the biggest disadvantages low-income kids face is often no one in their family is familiar with the application process and able to help.

However, make no mistake: it is the teen who is applying. Colleges are not accepting the parent, after all.

Again, we must ask, how does this way of talking impact the teen who hears it? In incredibly subtle ways, it reinforces the idea that they are not yet ready for this kind of responsibility. That they are not capable when it comes to the most pressing thing in their life. That at the time they most want free from their parents, they are stuck to them like glue. It's not a pretty message. I think if more parents realized this, they would pause.

I've heard the argument that if you say to the teen that "you're applying to college," it will make them feel as if they have to do it all on their own. I understand that possibility, and it's clearly not good either.

That's why it is important to both 1) give the teen space for their work *and* 2) reiterate your support. You can say to your teen, for example, "Your dad and I are happy to help you as you apply to college." Or, to others, "Our daughter is applying to colleges this year. There's a lot we all have to figure out!"

If we want children to be able to stand on their own, to feel good about their effort and accomplishments, to learn from their mistakes, and to take responsibility for their actions, we need to give them the space to have what is theirs. Pronoun abuse bleeds into this in subtle ways. I have heard many masterful teachers point this one out, and I have observed thousands of parents both in classrooms and out-of-classroom settings. Parents who maintain better boundaries do not use the *we* pronoun when describing their children's lives.

Things to Try

1. Just listen when children's work is being talked about. Listen to yourself and to those around you. Notice when you hear the pronoun-abusing *we* creep in.

2. The next time you hear a clear *we* violation by a parent, really stop to think about what the implicit message is, whether about or to the child.

3. Make a conscious decision to shift to using *you* when talking to the child about their own life and work.

We/You, Part 2

So is it ever appropriate to use the plural? It is, and it depends on the context.

We is a plural. So when we want to establish a sense of shared involvement or shared responsibility, *we* is both appropriate and helpful. This is especially true in classrooms. I use *we* all the time when I'm inviting my undergrads to share about their lives. Even in my 125-person classes, there's a lot of classroom discussion. On any given day, I have students talk to a neighbor, crank around in their chairs to make a small group, or talk as a whole classroom, myself included. One of the marvelous things about teaching at San Jose State is that I can count on lots of diverse life experiences in my classes—which is great when what you're teaching is child development!

When I throw a question out to the class, I tend to open with things like, "How many of us . . . ?" For example, when discussing the impact of being bilingual or multilingual, I might ask, "How many of us speak more than one language?" Lots of hands go up, and the whole class can see very quickly what proportion of the room shares that experience. Sometimes it's merely interesting to see, but often it's illuminating to them to learn that so many other people shared their childhood experiences. It reinforces the idea that childhood is varied, and introduces a human element at the same time.

Using *us* instead of *you*, I position myself right along with my students as a member of our learning community. It's a small shift, and some might say its disingenuous. I'm not, after all, saying that they are all equal with me or that my authority for the class doesn't exist. What I hope to do, though, is to signal that we are all in this space to learn and ask questions.

By using *us* in these cases, I offer myself as a co-participant. I do share things about myself, and I'll raise my hand along with the students to indicate particulars of my background. For example, when we talk about family structure, I'll raise my own hand for questions like, "Which of us are youngest kids in our families?" and "How many of us lived with our grandparents in the home?"

My intention here is to create a more comfortable space for sharing, and ultimately a stronger learning environment. I find that when my students see me as a learner alongside them, they connect with me more as an instructor and are willing to invest more effort into their own learning. Plus, it's a lot more fun for us all!

There can also be good reasons for parents to use *we*. My friend Dan worked his way out of using *we* in most cases, but he also found there were times when he *chose* to use it. One example was when his son Tony was badly concussed. Tony's recovery was very slow, and he missed a lot of school. Dan found that as his son was healing, there were times he used *we* intentionally to reassure Tony that he *wasn't* on his own and that his parents were there to help him through a very difficult time.

Understanding how pronoun abuse slips in, Dan navigated his son's recovery deliberately, using *we* to reassure, and *you* to signal what was truly Tony's work to do. Dan recognized where the boundaries were and set his language accordingly. He told me: "His mom and I can't do the work for him. We will be there to answer questions, to help coordinate the mountain of make-up work with his teachers, and to negotiate on his behalf, when needed. But the getting down to business and doing the make-up work are really up to him."

Used appropriately, *we* and *us* can create a sense of camaraderie and a shared sense of working together. Used inappropriately, they can signal lack of trust in a child's autonomy. It comes down to noticing when we should be involved and when we need to make space for children to have their own experience.

Things to Try

1. Notice when you say *we* or *us* to create a sense of shared purpose or endeavor. Notice how it feels to you and how it's received.

2. When working with teens, who value their independence so highly, try using *we* sparingly so that it can seep in when you do use it.

3. With young children, use *we* to generate enthusiasm and playfulness; for example, *Let's get our coats on; we can go outside now!*

10

Compelling Research

A closer look at four areas

A note before we dig in here. In writing this book, I have intentionally drawn on multiple areas of evidence: research, classroom practice, and family life stories. I think it helps to see the points of the book play out in all these areas. This chapter looks more closely at some of the research. I've chosen four areas that I believe are highly pertinent to how we talk to children, and I lay out just how strongly the research shows that talk shapes what children think.

In this chapter, I introduce and discuss the areas of parent-child reminiscing, metacognition, cognitive demand, and gender differences. We will see the impact of how we speak to children when talking about the past, when talking about our own thinking processes, in how much thinking is required by our talk, and in differences we are typically unaware of when speaking to boys or girls.

Parent-Child Reminiscing

It's clear that how parents talk has a direct impact on the patterns, behaviors, thoughts, and memories that kids have around their own past.

Have you ever wondered how children learn about the past? Specifically, *their* past? How do they come to understand that they are unique, quirky, wonderful individuals? Or that the two-year-old who drew on the walls is the same person who graduated from elementary school with a love of art? How do we build our understanding of who we are and how that person is continuous across time?

This area of research is known as *autobiographical* memory—namely, the memory we hold about ourselves. The two pioneers of this area, Robin Fivush and Katherine Nelson, began their studies of it in the late 1980s (eg, Fivush & Fromoff, 1988; Nelson, 1993). Research into autobiographical memory over the past thirty years has homed in on parent-child talk about the past. It's called *parent-child reminiscing*: talking about and revisiting personal history. This can be around shared family events or anything that the child has experienced.

In a nutshell, researchers have found that when parents have more conversations with their children about past events, those children have:

- Better self-concept and elaborated autobiographical memory
- A better understanding of the past, present, and future and of how they are connected

While any talk is better than none, the type of talk also matters. Specifically, parent-child reminiscing that is more highly *elaborative* has the biggest effects. I'll explain more, but first let's take a look at what it sounds like to talk to kids about their past.

My husband's family are big pie makers, and my mother-in-law's apple pie is divine. My own childhood family were more cake bakers. About the only pie my mom ever made was pumpkin pie for Thanksgiving, but it was delicious! One year when my kids were little, my mom was with us for Thanksgiving. She and my husband decided to try out each other's recipes, which our kids found hilarious!

Months later, in the kitchen making pie, I asked my children: "Do you remember when Grammy made Papa's apple pie and Papa made Grammy's pumpkin pie?"

"Mmhmm."

"Wasn't that funny?"

"Mmhmm!"

"What happened then?"

And they were off and running, talking about how it had gone and what they remembered and what they thought about it. We talked for several minutes about the pies and my mother's visit, about other things we did that Thanksgiving, and even a bit about our family's traditions for Thanksgiving in general.

I first set the stage for them to recall this special event, then asked them a simple yes-no question to begin with, and followed it with an open-ended question. This got them talking up a storm! It was a lovely conversation, and it prompted my kids to think a lot about special family time and their role in it.

Parent-child reminiscing doesn't have to be about special occasions or holidays. You can talk about everyday things just as easily. Trips to the grocery store, something that happened in preschool, or even just a walk around the block. All can be a launching point for conversations between parents and children that will cause the child to recall their memory of the event.

While most families do this kind of reminiscing talk, not all do, and there is some variation cross-culturally. Initially, the research on this focused on conversations with very young children. Since women are usually the primary caregivers of young children, most of the research on parent-child reminiscing has focused on what mothers do. The early research focused on upper middle-class white mothers, however the field has expanded considerably. The key results have been replicated widely in other US populations and also cross-culturally in other parts of the world. There's a lot of variation in how mothers talk to their children, even when comparing women within the same demographic group.

It's quite clear from thirty years of research that mothers vary in how much they do what's called *elaborative reminiscing*. Recall that elaboration is the idea of connecting new material to what you already know. Elaborative reminiscing describes the past in rich details, usually by including the child's recollection through a series of back-and-forth and open-ended questioning.

It's also clear from these decades of research that there is a huge connection between this kind of parent talk and what children come to understand.

Relationships have been seen between mothers' elaborative reminiscing style and children's autobiographical memory, their strategic memory, various language or literacy skills, and how a child comes to understand themselves, others, and the mind.

What we say to kids most definitely shapes what they think.

Research into parent-child elaborative reminiscing comes out of a Vygotskian tradition that views what humans do as learning in interaction. It matters, then, what kinds of conversations children take part in. And of course those conversations are informed by the prevailing values of the culture and the specific values of the family.

Some families spend more time talking about the past. Children in those families learn to do that more often, and better.

But they are learning more than just how to talk about the past. They're learning who they are.

In their review of the research literature published in *Child Development* in 2006, pioneer Robyn Fivush and colleagues Catherine Haden and Elaine Reese explain the impact this way: "By discussing, evaluating, and interpreting our past, we are engaging in self-reflection and understanding; by constructing personal narratives, we are constructing a sense of self through time, as related to others, yet each with a unique personal history" (2006, 1572).

People's understanding of themselves begins in early childhood. Humans all form autobiographical memory. Part of that memory is shaped by the autobiographical narratives we tell—to ourselves and to others. A *narrative* in this sense is more than a story that simply records or reports the past. Autobiographical narratives put the story into a larger context (of the family or the individual's life), and they include the importance of that story to that person's life.

There are two big differences in how mothers talk to their children about the past. The first is fairly obvious: some mothers offer a lot more detail about past events. They talk more and describe more, and they invite their children to do that too. The second difference is less obvious and also more important: some mothers ask more questions. In particular, they ask open-ended questions that create the opportunity for children to add their own ideas and details, as well as become more active participants in the story production.

The obvious outcome is that children whose mothers do this with them when they are little are more likely as older kids to talk more about their past and to do so in more detail. That makes sense. We learn what we practice.

What is more interesting, I think, is *all the other places* mothers' elaborative reminiscing shows up in their children's thinking. Three main outcome areas have been studied:

1. Strategic Memory (the use of strategies for remembering and planning to remember)

How well we remember things depends on many factors. One of the most important is whether we learn, and use, strategies to make remembering easier.

Young children whose mothers use an elaborative style of reminiscing do better on this. In studies where children are brought into a research lab and asked to do recall tasks, the kids who have been brought up with elaborative reminiscing are better able to master sets of objects to recall, and more likely to use strategies like naming the objects. Use of a strategy—any strategy—is a deliberate action that shows an intention or plan to remember. This is high-level cognitive work, especially for young children. Studies have shown that for children at forty-two months, fifty-four months, and sixty months of age, mothers' elaborative reminiscing style predicts their recall success.

In other words, talking to children more often about their past experiences, doing so in ways that include rich detail, and asking children to contribute to those conversations in open-ended ways improves both their memory generally and their strategic use of memory. Wow!

2. Language/Literacy Development

Parent-child reminiscing is a language-based activity, so it makes sense that it would impact a child's language development. It's a pretty easy bet that the rich detail in elaborative reminiscing translates to better vocabularies, and it does. It also promotes more complex language skills generally, which also makes sense.

But something more is going on, too. In recalling the past, parents draw their child's attention to something that is not happening in that present moment. They are asking the child to draw on a memory—a mental representation—and to think about it and talk about it. Where else do we do that? In books.

Children whose parents use more elaborative reminiscing have better print understanding skills—even before they can read. What we say shapes what and how kids think.

3. Understanding of the Human Mind

Human minds are messy and complicated—and invisible. Precisely because they are internal to a person's experience, they are hard for young children to make sense of. (There's a whole area of developmental psychology devoted to how children come to understand the human mind, called Theory of Mind.)

Because elaborative reminiscing includes talking about the importance of the story, it often includes discussion of feelings and internal states. Talking about these *in relation to a past event* places the emotions into context of what happened—which helps children make sense of emotions. And in fact, elaborative parent-child reminiscing shows up in children's later having a more robust understanding of themselves and their emotional experience. Kids emerge with a more coherent self-concept.

What's wild about this is that you'd think *any* discussion of emotions would lead kids to understand them better. But compared to emotional talk during storybook reading and emotional talk during reminiscing—only the reminiscing actually predicted kids' emotion understanding later.

I suspect that it's the anchoring of it in the child's life that makes the difference. Hooking a new way of thinking about emotion to their own preexisting memory seems like a powerful way to build *understanding*. There is even intriguing research connecting elaborative reminiscing with preschoolers to their later emotion *regulation* in their tweens.

So the research has shown clear links between this kind of elaborative reminiscing by parents and all kinds of ways that kids think. And it also points out ways these conversations build and strengthen bonds between the parent and child.

Overall, the research suggests this kind of reminiscing is good for kids. That makes sense: it invites language-intensive, emotionally rich discussion about the child's life. There is the possibility that the research base—still somewhat heavy in US populations and white families—is missing something. I don't see how it could hurt to have these conversations, though, and in my own parenting, I find that they are lovely to have.

Things to Try

1. The next time you're at the park with a child, ask them about a previous fun visit—get them talking about what they did then.

2. Before a family get-together, start a conversation about other times the child has shared with those family members. Encourage the child to recall as much as they can about things they've enjoyed together.

3. When reading with a child or group of children, ask when they have done something like what happens in the book.

Metacognitive Talk

One of the areas that speaks strongly to the notion that how we talk to kids shapes their thinking is the area of *metacognitive talk*. It will help to lay out a bit about metacognition here, and then I can get at how what we say does (or doesn't) build it for kids.

What Is Metacognition?

Metacognition is usually defined as "thinking about thinking," but in my field (Learning Sciences) that definition gets extended. Instead, **metacognition is the ability not only to think about your thinking, but to *evaluate* it.** The key here is the evaluation piece because it's in realizing that our knowledge is lacking, or inadequate, that we can see where we need to grow and hopefully even how we might go about learning what we need to know.

Metacognition is the gateway to success. Experts are the pinnacle of using it. It's not just that they know a lot about their topic (which they do), it's that they can recognize quickly what they don't yet understand, and they can act in ways to correct that.

When people are able to reflect metacognitively, they are no longer bound to the facts that they hold but can flexibly apply their understanding to new situations. That adaptability is the hallmark of intelligence.

Without exception, the material I teach on metacognition is of great interest to my upper division classes. These seniors are in their last year of college and getting ready to move out into their professions. Prior to my class, they usually have brushed up against the term, but they have no real understanding of it. They certainly have no appreciation for how ubiquitous the skill is, or how powerful. At the end of the semester, when I ask students to reflect on a single idea that they will take away with them in their teaching or parenting, metacognition shows up prominently.

What's Involved in Metacognition?

The process of metacognition involves three main components: prior knowledge, self-regulation, and reflection.

1. Prior Knowledge

Whenever we work on something, we bring our existing knowledge with us into the activity. But there are many aspects to what we "know":

- The relevant content (for example, math, history, sewing, 3D printing, etc.)
- The task at hand or type of problem, including similar problems
- What we know about ourselves—including how we learn, react, and work

2. Self-regulation

In thinking metacognitively, we learn to focus on our own knowledge; we learn to self-monitor—predicting our success as we get started, monitoring our progress along the way, and correcting our understanding as we go. These are self-regulatory actions. You can see how a learner engaged in these types of actions is going to draw a lot more from what they're doing.

3. Reflection

Unfortunately, this last step is the one most likely to be left out. It is the hardest and also the most crucial.

When we reflect, we look at our own level of understanding—at how it has changed, at what has limited us, and at where we'd like to go next. It is reflection that leads to insight and new understanding.

If you've ever had a debriefing meeting after a big project, you may have seen that reflecting on how things went helped the group to consolidate its lessons and progress, and to plan for even better performance in the future. In my experience, very few project groups actually make the time to reflect, though. They tend to wrap up and move on.

It's the same with kids. If they aren't asked to reflect, it is highly unlikely that they will stumble onto doing so on their own. And if you do have the rare child who does this, you'll likely find that they are incredibly frustrated by standard schooling, which usually makes no room for it at all.

How is Metacognition Learned?

So metacognition is a terrific and powerful learning tool. It enables us to think about what we're doing and evaluate whether it's working well or what more we might need. But Learning Science has also found that metacognition cannot be taught in isolation as a set of skills or steps. **Metacognitive skills can *only* be learned in the service of other activities.** They must be embedded in what people are doing in order to be learned and mastered.

To go one step further, metacognitive skills don't have to be explicitly taught at all. They just have to be employed and modeled.

Here's an example. In his 2016 book *Helping Children Succeed*, Paul Tough talks about skills he's identified as being important for kids to succeed, including qualities like "grit, curiosity, self-control, optimism, and conscientiousness" (2016, 9). Like many journalists today, Tough refers to these skills or qualities as "non-cognitive," a term that makes absolutely no sense given that thinking permeates all of them.

In the book, Tough talks about an inner city chess teacher whose low-income students learned not only chess, but also important skills such as perseverance, resiliency in the face of loss, and a willingness to work toward future goals. They learned these things while playing the game. Tough was puzzled by the ability of the children to absorb these additional lessons without explicit instruction in them. It led him to question whether the metaphor of "teaching" is the right way to go about thinking about inculcating these skills. It led him, ultimately, to thinking about a child's environment and how that environment is set up.

Tough says the chess teacher, Elizabeth Spiegel, never used "words like *grit* or *character* or *self-control*" nor did she give mini-motivational speeches. Tough describes it this way: "Instead, her main pedagogical technique was to intensely analyze the mistakes they had made, helping them see what they could have done differently. Something in her careful and close attention to her students' work changed not only their chess ability but also their approach to life" (2016, 10). And Tough noticed that what Spiegel was *saying* to the kids was having a profound impact on how they *thought*.

What Tough *doesn't* recognize is that Spiegel's coaching was leading her students through an exercise in metacognition. By drawing their attention to what they had done and how it could be done better, she was helping them build the capacity to self-monitor and self-correct. She didn't need to label these skills or try to teach them—they were available through the interaction, through what she said to them. And because these skills were available, they guided the students toward greater competency in their chess playing. That's how metacognition works. It shows us what to pay attention to. It helps us improve, deepen our understanding, and build new thinking faster.

And all of this—whether in classrooms like Elizabeth Spiegel's, or homes like mine—is accomplished through language. How we speak to kids—how we structure the questions we ask and the feedback we give—can be tailored to build them toward the kinds of thinking involved in metacognition: drawing on their prior knowledge, self-regulating, and reflecting.

Parenting and Metacognitive Talk

Some parents and teachers embed metacognitive skills intuitively. When they are working with children, they naturally invite them into reflection. They talk about how to approach a task or why a particular strategy might help. They explain how things work or ask the child to think about it. This kind of talk supports children building their own metacognition.

My favorite study on parenting and metacognitive support comes from researchers Carol Neitzel and Anne Stright at Indiana University. They looked at how children and their mothers interacted during the summer before the children started kindergarten and then at how the children did in class during their kindergarten year. They found very tight correlations between the ways that mothers spoke to their children during problem-solving activities at home and how their children navigated kindergarten.

Their 2003 study looked at sixty-eight preschooler-mother pairs (the majority were white, but with a huge range in mothers' level of education, spanning from less than high school to graduate degree). They wanted to see how mothers helped their children and specifically how the *type* of help might be related to how the children did in kindergarten. They tracked what mothers said and coded it for support along three lines: metacognition, emotional support, and autonomy. Metacognitive talk was measured as information offered explaining how the task worked, about the task management techniques or strategies, or rationale for using a particular strategy.

In the first phase of the study, each preschooler-mother pair was visited in their home and asked to work together on four intentionally difficult problem-solving activities: reconstructing a shape following only verbal instructions, building a block tower, planning a bear's birthday party, and making up a story using a set of six puppets. The researchers designed the activities to be beyond the child's ability so that the mother would need to help in some way.

In the second phase of the study, each child was observed twice during their kindergarten year. What Neitzel and Stright found was that *the way* mothers talked to their children correlated closely with all kinds of subsequent behaviors their children had in the classroom. What is powerful about this study is that the researchers were able to isolate specific kinds of talk and the impact those had on children's thinking and behavior later, in the classroom. Notice that these classroom skills look remarkably like Paul Tough's list of skills that kids need to be successful, namely "grit, curiosity, self-control, optimism, and conscientiousness"!

Specifically, Neitzel and Stight found these links between how mothers talked to their children and what their children did later in class:

1. *Mothers who offered more metacognitive talk and adjusted the difficulty of task* had children who did more metacognitive talk and monitored their progress more.

2. *Mothers who offered more emotional support of children's problem solving* had children who were more likely to seek help in the classroom.

3. *Mothers who offered more emotional support of children's problem solving* and *autonomy* had children who were persistent and self-controlled in the classroom.

The language these children had exposure to and practice with at home showed up in their classroom work in kindergarten. What we say really does shape how kids think.

Things to Try

1. Listen to how you talk to children when they are working on something new or difficult. Do you explain how the task works or discuss strategies and why they might help?

2. If this is newer for you, the next time you're working with a child on a problem-solving activity, try to offer two specific strategies for managing the task.

3. If this kind of talk is common for you, bump it up from telling to asking. Prompt the child to think about how the task might work or to think about what approach would help.

Cognitive Demand (Boys Hear It More)

We can all agree that if you practice something, you get better at it. And if you don't practice, how can you have the opportunity to improve?

So it's important to know that **boys are getting different opportunities to think more deeply and explore the world.** This can be seen in a research lab setting and also out in the real world.

Cognitive demand is the term for how much thinking is required of us. Open-ended questions, for example, require more than a simple yes/no, and so they are more cognitively demanding. Being asked to explain, or to consider someone else's explanation, or to think about the future or the past, or to reconstruct an idea—all of these involve high cognitive demand.

When I was in graduate school, I learned about how differently parents speak to their boys than their girls. I wondered what longer-term impacts it would have on the kinds of questions and thinking that the children had.

In a terrific simple research design, Cam Leaper at UC Santa Cruz found that parents say different kinds of things to their sons versus their daughters—even when the kids are playing with the same toys (e.g., Leaper, 2002). Leaper and his graduate students attempted to recreate the kinds of interactions parents might have at their homes. They had parents come to the lab—a nice living-room setting—and play with three different toys: a tea party (typically for girls), a set of trucks (typically for boys), and a zoo set (gender neutral). They recorded what and how much the parents said. They found that parents, both mothers and fathers, asked more questions while playing with the girl-stereotyped toy but that these questions were fairly simple and conversational.

The harder, more complex questions—the ones that involved more thinking, or *cognitive demand*—were asked when playing with the boy-stereotyped toy. And they found that both mothers and fathers asked those questions more of their sons than their daughters.

Maureen Callanan, also at UC Santa Cruz, went to a local children's science museum to look at how parents talked to their children. She and Kevin Crowley found that as families moved through the museum, parents all talked to their kids; in fact both mothers and fathers spoke fairly equally to their daughters and sons about how to engage with the exhibit. What was markedly different, though, was that parents were *three times more likely* to explain *the science* to their sons. The research team also found that both mothers and fathers asked harder questions and gave more detailed explanations to their sons. This was true independent of 1) how long the family spent at a given exhibit, and 2) the interest or questions asked by the child!

One huge complication in terms of cognitive demand is that from very early on—in infancy, in most cases—we give kids gender-stereotyped toys. And the research on child gender and parenting finds that parents encourage gender-specific play.

Those toys encourage different kinds of playing—and talking. Toys for girls invite chatting. In the research literature, it's referred to as *affiliative, cooperative play*. Toys for boys don't do that. Boys' toys invite doing things and constructing, referred to as *instrumental, problem-solving play*. When parents talk to their kids in their gender-specific play activities they reinforce the patterns of talk. Boys' toys invite more problem-solving language, and parents' relationships with their boys lead them to encourage more of that talk. This is compounded by the finding that parents tell girls what to do more than they tell their boys.

At the heart of this is the difference in cognitive demand—in the level of effort required to think about or solve a given task. The easiest level of demand is a recall test, for example:

- At home—Do you remember when Grandma visited and we made apple pie?
- At school—Who can tell me the capital of Georgia?
- At the park—Where's our stuff?
- In preschool—What color is this?

Recall questions just rehash what we've already seen and heard. This type of question just asks kids to go into their heads and pull out a fact that they already learned. It's not that hard. It's also not that interesting. (Think of it this way: would you rather eat a fresh-cooked meal or reheated leftovers?) Asking recall questions doesn't exercise children's brains very much, and it certainly doesn't add that much to their understanding. It isn't building anything new and fresh.

Questions that ask kids to really think require higher levels of cognitive demand, asking them to make connections or create new ideas. This is meatier stuff. It's way more fun and way more interesting. And it leads to much better learning. This is the power of *elaboration*, which I introduced in Chapter 5, "Shifting the Language of Control."

When kids make connections between new things they see and what they already understand, it does two things:

1. It deepens their understanding of the prior information.

2. It increases the chance that they will understand, and also remember, the new stuff.

Building networks of interconnected ideas is the foundation of deep understanding. In general, we're not doing well by kids in this regard. But we're shortchanging our girls the most.

What this means is that starting as early as preschool, without any idea that we're doing it, we talk to our boys in ways that helps them develop an inquiring mind, and we talk to our girls in a way that is less likely to do so. Throughout grade school, kids have much the same scores in math and science—in fact, girls may have a slight edge in terms of grades. But by middle school, there is a sharp drop-off of girls from math and science. They feel it's not for them, and they lose interest. A lot of work is being done to understand why this change occurs and how school curriculum might be changed to keep girls motivated in science. I have to wonder though, if we held them to the same level of cognitive demand, whether we would see the drop-off.

Even just the *presence* of boy-stereotyped toys has been found to correlate (for both boys and girls) to later school achievement. Successful female scientists and mathematicians speak about how strong an influence their family was, providing the resources and support that helped them pursue their interests and to believe that they could do anything they wanted.

Things to Try

1. Listen for the ways you speak to children. Are you asking them questions? What sort of answers do those questions invite?

2. Try asking a kind of question you don't use very often, for example, asking the child an open-ended question or to explain how something works.

3. Look for opportunities to connect what the child is doing to ideas you think they already understand. Ask them how things are connected!

Gender Differences and Mathematics

Cognitive demand is one area where gender differences in how adults speak to boys and girls have been found, but there are many, many others. Differences can be found in the amount of talk, in the kinds of topics, in the amount of talk about emotions, and in the kinds and amount of scaffolding done by parents, just for a start. Because it is highly significant to girls' future career success, I want to discuss the research on gender, language, and mathematics.

Stereotyped Language Starts at Birth—or Earlier

One idea that always captivates my students is how early gender stereotyping starts. It's no secret that babies come into a world that is already color coded for them. We all know that when parents-to-be find out the sex of their baby, people want to give them things that are the "right" color. Don't know the sex of the baby? Better stick to green or yellow. Even purple has been co-opted for girls.

But most of us are unaware of how we *talk* to a newborn baby.

When I started teaching I heard about a study done with newborns that showed this beautifully. The *same baby* was wrapped in either a pink blanket or a blue blanket, and the people taking part in the study were invited to hold it. People holding the "boy" baby tended to hold it farther from their body, more loosely, and even bounced it around a bit. They spoke to it in deeper, rougher tones. They spoke about the "boy" being big, and tough, and a man some day.

People holding the "girl" baby tended to hold it closer to their bodies, more securely, more gingerly. They spoke in softer, quieter, higher-pitched tones. And they spoke about being beautiful, pretty, and small.

Acting this out for my students captures their attention and catches them by surprise. They are astonished that we start separating kids that early—essentially as soon as they're born.

My students go on to question what else they might be doing differently, with nieces and nephews, for example, based on gender. And then to question what they are doing with boys and girls in general. They start to see that we create the environments children grow up in—and that our words are a huge part of that.

So What?

It's not the differences per se that I'm interested in here though. It's making clear the connection between what we say to kids and how that shapes what they think.

One place getting attention these days is the area of mathematics. Because math is a gateway to the sciences, engineering, and high-paying professional careers, math is a big-stakes subject for kids. And it's becoming clear that how we talk to girls and boys is creating a gender difference that favors boys.

The *Huffington Post* featured a story in 2016 about a study examining whether the gender gap in mathematics has lessened any in recent years. Looking at scores for over twelve thousand students who were kindergartners in either 1999 or 2011, researchers found that, in fact, the gap persists. Specifically, they were able to see that the gap in scores starts as early as kindergarten, that it starts at the highest performing levels, and that it quickly spills out to all levels of achievement. By second and third grade, the gap in performance between boys and girls is already deeper and more pervasive. And even worse, the study also showed that teachers consistently score girls lower even when they have the same tested math achievement and the same observable behaviors in class.

These differences hadn't budged from 1999 to 2011.

That's a big deal.

The study's lead author, Joseph Cimpian, shared a story about one of the teachers they approached at the start of their research. This teacher was indignant that the scientists were even *looking* for gender differences. She went to the point of bringing in her grade sheets to prove to them there was no gender difference in her classroom. She hotly justified her protest to the researchers with, "That's because girls can perform as well as boys if they try hard enough."

Cimpian then describes this beautiful moment that followed—as the teacher realized the implications of what she had just said. She had truly believed there were no biases in her grading. She had truly believed that these researchers would see that when they looked at her grade book and saw that girls were among the high performers. But she had not seen within herself that this belief masked the idea that girls could only achieve comparably "if they tried hard enough." In the wake of catching her own conflict, the teacher retracted her protest and even lent her weight to the need for the study.

It takes a lot to hear ourselves and to be honest enough to catch ourselves. I'm incredibly impressed by this teacher.

In the study itself, which was published in October 2016 in *AERA Open*, the researchers discuss possible sources for the achievement gap between boys and girls. What could be the explanation behind the data? How is it that even when girls and boys have the same test scores and the same kinds of classroom behavior, their teachers consistently grade them below the boys?

The researchers say their study points to the idea that "teachers must perceive girls as working harder than similarly achieving boys in order to rate them as similarly proficient in math." Just like the teacher with her grade sheets did.

Think about that: girls have to work harder than boys just to earn the same grade. And we start doing that to them *in kindergarten*. When they're five! And then we wonder why girls don't see themselves as good at math or why they aren't interested in engineering.

It brings to mind the famous quote attributed to cartoonist Bob Thaves, about the legendary dancing duo Fred Astaire and Ginger Rogers: "Sure he was great, but don't forget, Ginger Rogers did everything he did backwards ... and in high heels!"

Consider again the teacher from the story who was so indignant. Despite her initial protests that her equal grades were proof of no gap, she saw that she held gender-biased beliefs. One wonders how those beliefs might have impacted her students.

This particular study looked at thousands of student scores but no actual classroom interactions. We have no direct account of how things were done in these classes. But do consider that the teacher who protested believed strongly that she was egalitarian. How was she able to glimpse otherwise? *Through her words.*

Teachers' behavior in the classroom reveals their expectations and biases, even when they themselves might not realize it. This has been known and studied for a long time. We know, for example, that teachers commonly allow more time in classrooms for boys to talk. They accept more disruptive behavior of boys. They ask boys more, and harder, questions. And, it seems, they grade them higher even when other evidence suggests equal talent. It is impossible for me to imagine that this wouldn't be coming out in how teachers speak to the class.

Not Just in Kindergarten

While working on this piece, I also happened to read an article in the *Atlantic* magazine called "Why Is Silicon Valley So Awful to Women?" The article examines why so many women leave high tech. It profiled several top female executives who shared their experiences of being treated by their male colleagues from disrespectfully to lecherously, or as if they were incompetent.

A comment by one of the women particularly caught my eye. It was from Tracy Chau, an engineer and one of the co-founders of Project Include. She was talking about specific examples and the general climate at a previous tech startup where she and the sole other female engineer felt "as if they were held to a different standard."

Maybe that doesn't sound like a big deal to you, but I was in the middle of writing this section about the gap in math scores. Listen to how it impacted the two women: "Not feeling like we were good enough to be there—even though, objectively speaking, we were." Objectively speaking. In other words, their coding skills and job performance were comparable.

Now look again at the results from the study on the gap in kindergarten math scores. Recall that the study shows teachers consistently score girls lower, even when they have the same tested math achievement and observable behaviors in class.

And look again at the conclusion drawn by the researchers, that teachers "must perceive girls **as working harder than similarly achieving boys in order to rate them as similarly proficient in math**" [bold is mine]. Even though, objectively speaking, they are as proficient. Sounds just like Tracy Chau's experience, doesn't it.

The importance of mathematics to so many wonderful and high-paying careers has led to more urgency in tackling the gender gap. One of the key math education experts on this is Jo Boaler, Stanford professor and founder of the YouCubed center at Stanford. Boaler is very vocal about making math accessible to girls (e.g., Boaler, 2002; Boaler & Sengupta-Irving, 2006). Quoted in an article on *CNN* in October 2016, Boaler decries both the myth of a math gene and especially the notion that boys are the ones who have it. She argues that talking about mathematics in this way influences what kids think. And it is a direct, measurable relationship. She says, "We know that when mothers tell their daughters 'I wasn't good at math in school,' their daughter's achievement goes down."

This hidden belief that boys are stronger at some things comes out in our words. It's not just in kindergarten, and it's not just in mathematics. It's in all of what we say—to both girls and boys. What we say shapes what kids think. And that follows them through their lives.

Things to Try

1. Listen to how the adults in your life talk to—and about—girls versus boys. What differences do you hear?

2. Try talking with a friend or colleague about this research. What aspects of it interest or trouble you the most? What does the other person think?

3. Pay attention to how you speak to children. Do you speak to both boys and girls (relatively) equally about doing/building and being capable?

11

What Not to Do

A few things we really should avoid

In general, it is my intention to offer this book as a guide, offering readers information about how the ways we talk to children are being received, and forming the child's understanding of the world. For the most part, I'm not interested in telling people what they're doing wrong.

This short chapter is the lone exception.

Here, I lay out a few things that are truly not a good idea to say, from talking about children within their own hearing to using excessive praise or shaming them, plus a laundry list of brief notes about other kinds of talk to avoid. Being aware of these can help us do the better job we all want to do for the children in our lives.

Talking *About* the Child

Often, adults talk *about* a child even when the child is right in front of them—about personal and private things, like body changes, or grades, or mistakes, or complaints about things the child has done. With the child right there. These are times when the child is the *subject* of the conversation but not really *part* of the conversation.

In speaking to friends and others about this, I've found this is something almost no one has given any thought to. It's incredibly common among parents, and also among teachers. I'd like to suggest that it is incredibly disrespectful. It's a power move, by which I mean it's the move of someone who has more power than the other person. How can you tell? Just ask how you'd feel if your spouse did this to you at a party: talked *about* you, with you right there, but not as a way to bring you into the conversation.

As always, ask, What is this teaching the child? Being spoken about within one's own hearing—especially if it is about sensitive issues—can do several things:

- It tends to make the child feel invisible, small, and ultimately resentful.
- It tells the child that they are an object.
- It sends the message that their feelings are irrelevant, or at least less important than the adult's.

If you are tempted to speak with another adult *about* a child in their presence, weigh the following before you speak:

- Why does the other person need to know this about the child?
- If there is a real need, is this something the child can tell them directly?
- If not, what can you say to the child as a preface?
- If there is no real need, could it wait till the child is out of earshot or even just not be shared?

Here's an example of how this can work. My sister-in-law is a pediatrician at a large city hospital. When she meets her young patients, she talks directly to the child, even if it's a young kid. She'll say things like, "Thanks for coming in to see me today. I see you brought someone with you—is this your mom? What brings you in today? Does anything hurt? Where does it hurt?"

Most of the time, the kids will answer her and start talking up a storm, but occasionally they're quiet and seem to hide behind their parent. If the doctor sees this and is unable to get them to warm up to her, she just asks the child, "Would you rather I ask these questions to your mom?" A nod or a yes and she switches over to addressing the adult.

In the process, what has the child learned?

- That the doctor cares what's wrong with them.
- That they have information that is valid for the doctor to know.
- That they can choose whether to talk or not.

Children are listening and learning whether we're speaking directly to them or about them. It's worth keeping that in mind and asking what we want them to be learning.

Things to Try

1. Listen for times that you or others talk about children in their presence. Observe the child to see what they seem to make of it. Do they look uncomfortable? Disengage? Act up?

2. If you are speaking about a very young child in their hearing, preface your comment, for example, with, "I need to let your teacher know about what happened today."

3. If you want to share something about a child while they are present, include them in the conversation; for example, "I loved what you did today at the library. I'm going to tell Carol about that."

No Praise

I often hear adults make comments like these to children:

"That picture is beautiful."
"You're really smart/beautiful/clever/etc."
"You're a natural at this."

Ask yourself—why would kids even need to hear these sorts of things?

All of this praise is misguided. It comes out of the self-esteem movement that got rolling in the 1980s—the idea that kids need to be propped up so that they can feel good about themselves. A generation before, no one did this. It's very recent, and it's not having a good effect on children and teens.

Now think about when you might have said something like that—what motivated it? Did you want to inspire the child to do well, or to do better?

Could it be that you had no idea what else to say?

When I hear this kind of empty praise, it tells me that the speaker has nothing of real merit to say to the child. In my undergraduate classes at SJSU, my students were required to perform twenty hours of service learning with infants, children, or youth. I routinely heard from my students that they didn't know what to say to the kids they were working with. This truly surprised me because most of my students have children in their lives—younger siblings, extended family, or even the children of friends. And yet, somehow, talking to a kid they didn't know made them clam up. Many of my students shared that they found themselves tongue-tied and that they just started complimenting the child on something. Some even expressed how grateful they were that the kid started talking to them first!

So in my classes, we talked about what kids are like and what you might say to them, and inevitably my students relaxed into their service learning experience. Each semester, virtually every student came out with a greater appreciation for what kids are like and an enjoyment for talking to them.

One of the reasons I loved teaching my giant lecture class was that I increased my sphere of influence—I could reach 125 young adults at one pop instead of just 30 or so. I'm hopeful that this book will continue that. Something has gone very wrong in our society that young adults feel they do not know how to talk to a child.

It's important to understand that praise of this sort—what I call *empty praise*—creates two problems for the child:

1. A fixed mindset—it focuses on success rather than learning, and the idea that success is innate—you have it or you don't.

2. External motivation—it focuses on other people's opinions.

First—the idea that success is a fixed quality. This goes directly to the work of Carol Dweck and her findings that when people hold a view that success and intelligence are innate, internal, genetic things, they don't fare as well. Praise pushes us into this viewpoint, which is clearly counterproductive if our goal is for children to build the capacity for lifelong success and contribution. Empty praise doesn't really help kids feel good about themselves. Sure, it might feel nice in the moment, a sort of fleeting dopamine hit. But it doesn't build real self-confidence. In fact, it's worse than that: it's actually unhelpful.

Second—external motivation. Counter to what people expect, praise actually kills motivation. When a child, teen, or adult does something they want to do and enjoy doing, they are internally motivated. Anything coming from the outside—a grade, a sticker, award, or praise—is an external reward. Decades of research on motivation have clearly determined that rewards kill internal motivation. The more you praise someone, the less they want to do, and enjoy doing, that very thing.

Internal and external motivation are a continuum. People have or follow both, but to different degrees and often for different types of goals and activities. You may be internally motivated to explore cooking and externally motivated to be the top sales agent in your company this quarter. There are clearly people who thrive on competition and winning, and for these folks, outside factors drive them to do more and to excel. That's not the norm though. The norm is for people to pursue things they are internally interested in. And rewards from someone else spoil that.

Empty praise also teaches kids to look for more praise. Even more problematically, it teaches kids to look outside themselves for evaluation. In my university classes, this trend is incredibly apparent. When I ask my students to critique their own work, they have no idea how to do it. Even with a rubric (a topic for another day, perhaps), most are often unable to assess the depth or completeness of their work.

Like many educators, I've relented to say that if you need to praise, at least praise the effort rather than the ability:

"You worked hard on that."
"You really stuck with it."

The deeper question though is why offer praise at all? Why do we feel the need to offer our evaluation—our judgment, really—of what children do? In terms of metacognition, why not use the moment instead as an opportunity to help the child build their own self-reflection?

So better even than praising effort would be to ask the child to self-evaluate. Ask them what they *think*:

"You got an A. What's the best part about that for you?"

Or talk about or ask how they are *feeling* rather than praise them:

"You got cast in the school play. You must be very happy!"

"You missed a lot of goals in the game today. You doing OK?"

Yes, this can feel awkward at first. Keep trying, and see what it reveals to you about the children you interact with.

Things to Try

1. Really, just listen at first. Try to notice how often you praise kids and notice what elicits that praise.

2. Think of a couple of variations that praise effort, that you can have in your back pocket. Then when you feel the urge to give "empty praise," try one of those instead. Notice how the child responds.

3. Bump it up and try to structure your interaction to encourage children to evaluate themselves. Notice how it feels to *you* to keep your evaluation out of it. Notice what the child is able to say about himself or herself.

No Shame

Shaming kids is not going to get you any place useful. I think we can all see this at face value, but I've heard teachers, school administrators, and parents say things like these:

> "What are you doing here?!"
> "What were you thinking?!"
> "Don't be stupid!"
> "Are you an idiot?!"
> "Are you sure you're related to your brother?!"

You might congratulate yourself for not speaking to kids and teens this way. Maybe you intuitively know it's not the way to speak to people. Here's why it's especially important for children.

As children grow, they build their *self-concept*—their understanding of who they are and what they're worth. Self-concept has been robustly described in the research literature and goes through a well-recognized developmental progression. Initially, very young children are able to identify simple, observable, and fairly concrete things about themselves, such as the fact that they are a girl, or have yellow hair, or love to run. By middle childhood (around age eight or nine), they start to define themselves in relation to others and in terms of characteristics, like being a little sister or being faster than their classmates.

In late childhood (around age eleven or twelve), children are able to think of themselves in terms of traits, such as being smart, or kind, or funny. The final layer gets set in adolescence, as teenagers build the nuance of understanding that their traits may vary from setting to setting. For example, they can know they are quiet at home but noisy with friends, or shy about standing out in class but eager to take a leadership role in sports.

Notice that across all these emerging ideas about self are *words*. Language infiltrates our very fiber. The words we have to work with will show up in how we think of ourselves. That means the words we give children will lead to their self-concept.

So what words are we using? And how is that translating to what kids think about themselves?

Brené Brown studies and speaks on the topics of shame and vulnerability. This 2007 quote from her is a powerful reminder for anyone who spends time with children: "Shame corrodes the very part of us that believes we are capable of change."

The part of us that believes we're capable of change. Think about this for a minute. Childhood is *defined* by change and development. Shaming a child/teen cuts off their best avenue for healthy growth.

Shame doesn't honor the other person's soul. How can we inspire anyone to greatness or to be their own best self if we use our words to break them down? How could convincing a child that they are less capable possibly be a good thing to do?

Shaming is dehumanizing. It tells the receiver that they are not worth as much as you, and that they would do well to model themselves after you in order to improve.

I get it—kids do unthinking, unwise, and yes, even stupid things. I've watched kids do them, my own children included. I think it's part of being human. And I am quite convinced it doesn't cease with childhood.

The question is how to respond when kids do something wrong? Here's an example from when my son was about six. We live in California, so it's easy to eat outside most of the year. And for a former Georgia girl the best part is no bugs!

We'd finished dinner and it was time to clear the table, which our kids have been responsible for since they were young. We don't have a big house or yard, but the trek from outside to the kitchen is definitely longer. My son was (almost) always happy to help, but he liked to limit the number of trips he made.

On this evening, he grabbed his plate with one hand, loaded up his silverware onto it, and hurried into the house. Not surprisingly, something went wrong. The silverware went crashing to the ground, food scattering from the plate onto the patio. This wasn't the first time it happened.

I could have yelled. I could have belittled him. Instead, what I did was:

1. Focus on the action, not the child.

"Wow. That really wasn't safe."

2. Identify the actual concern.

"When you run with your plate like that, you could slip like you just did. If you trip, it can make a mess, or you could get hurt. Or something might get broken."

3. Ask for what I wanted to have happen instead.

"Please walk when you're clearing the table. And please carry the plate using both hands."

4. Support how he could fix the problem he had created.

"Grab a paper towel while you're in the kitchen so you can clean up the spill."

The question worth asking is, was what I said effective? To see that, let's go back to what I was trying to teach in the moment:

- Safety
- Responsibility
- Good humor

Let's be perfectly honest. Nothing you say to kids is going to work with only one shot. This wasn't the first time something like this had happened. Nor was it the last night our son tried to carry his plate one-handed. (He's convinced he can do it safely.)

What I was doing was laying a foundation—for better choices in the future. For his attention to be on what he's doing when he carries his plate in. And for him to be prepared when things go wrong to be both willing and able to solve the problem.

When I speak to my kids, I want the words I use to help them address the concern in the short term and also to prepare them for better living in the future. And I want them to be without shame because that just gets in the way of building a positive sense of capability.

Was I successful? I'd say yes. Our son doesn't get yelled at for making mistakes, he is quite willing in principle to help out around the house, and he hardly ever balks at cleaning up a mess he makes. He's not a model of perfection, but he is a good kid who can be relied on most of the time. I call that a win.

Things to Try

1. Bite back any snippy comment you feel coming out of you toward a child. Just that. Simply not doing damage is a fine start.

2. The next time you feel frustrated by what a child or teen is doing, try identifying your concern and say that to the child. What kind of response do you get?

3. Next time, try to phrase the concern in a positive way and add in the information about what you would like instead. See if the child understands and agrees to work on that with you.

What Else We Don't Say

Not shaming kids is fairly easy to understand. There are other, less obvious, places where our words are having a negative impact on children's thinking. I'd like to highlight a few other common kinds of talk and why it's a good idea to avoid them.

Threats

Threats may work in the short term, but they don't work to change behavior. Sure, threats can get the child to stop at the time. The test is whether kids will follow the rules when you aren't present. Too many parents, caregivers, and even teachers seem not to remember being kids themselves. Threats just push the behavior underground, where you can't see it or protect the child. And on top of that, you lose the opportunity to influence them because you damage the relationship.

Insulting Language

Insulting language is never a good idea. It's demeaning. It's also not teaching kids to be impeccable with their words. They see the adult getting to speak like this and know they are not allowed to. As with *please* and *thank you*, kids see this as one more place adults are held to a different standard, and they rebel against it.

Gossip

Gossip—just *why*? Bad-mouthing others is a way to make ourselves feel better. When we talk about others behind their back, what we're saying is that we ourselves feel small. It teaches children to be small-minded and unkind. As Brené Brown, shame and vulnerability researcher, commented in a 2012 interview with Jennifer Kogan in the *Washington Post*: "First and foremost, we need to be the adults we want our children to be. We should watch our own gossiping and anger. We should model the kindness we want to see."

Listening to the radio in the car recently with my teenage daughter, the radio DJ introduced a social media story saying, "Oh, I sure wouldn't want to be this girl. She was at a museum and—" I flipped to another station, asking out loud "Why? Why would I want to revel in someone else's misfortune?" My daughter agreed, "No reason at all." What we say to kids goes in.

Comparisons to Other Kids

Comparing a child to other kids—whether a sibling, a classmate, or some other child—is unhelpful. It teaches children that we think they're not as valuable as other people.

Around the age of eight, children begin to notice how they stack up to their peers. They start doing what's called *social comparison,* a natural part of self-concept development. Social comparison helps kids come to understand themselves, their likes and dislikes, and their capabilities, from "I'm stronger than him" to "I'm good at art."

There's a difference between children drawing comparisons *for themselves* and an adult drawing those comparisons. In their classic *Siblings Without Rivalry*, Adele Faber and Elaine Mazlish even devote an entire chapter to the "perils of comparison"!

When we compare kids, it's usually to show shortcoming— the "Why can't you be more like your sister/friend?" sort of comments. The flip side is just as dangerous to children's healthy development though. Being told that they're better than other children puts kids on a path to arrogance, fixed mindset, and a reliance on finding value outside themselves. It's akin to praise, but worse because it pits children against others in order to perceive and attain their sense of self-worth.

The world is full of people, and the beautiful thing is we all excel at and are drawn to different things. It's not a problem to notice these. What is a problem is to make someone feel worse—or better—on the basis of those comparisons.

Diet or Fat

I strike up conversations with people frequently. In a coffeeshop while writing this book I met a pediatric nurse who specializes in eating disorders for a world-class hospital. As you might imagine, I had a lot of questions for her! I had heard that clinicians are seeing more boys than before. She confirmed that trend, as well as two others that I find incredibly disturbing. The age of kids with eating disorders has dropped precipitously—patients as young as eight and nine are entering their program! Clinics are also seeing eating disorders in new populations—low-income kids and Latino and African-American kids.

Where is this coming from? It would be too simple to say it's how parents talk at home or how teachers talk at school. But certainly those venues have an influence. It's clear that some significant component to eating disorder behavior is genetic. I've seen estimates anywhere from 50 percent to 80 percent, depending on the study. But that means at least 20 percent—and maybe up to 50 percent—is *not* genetic. And that's where what we say to kids has an influence. When mothers talk about dieting or being fat, their daughters (and now also their sons) are listening and being impacted—making them more likely to develop an eating disorder.

Talking about food and nutrition is important to do with kids—at home and school. We want to help kids establish a healthy relationship with food. Talk about food as fuel; explain why we need a variety of nutrients and to eat well. It may be an uphill battle against marketing and social media, but at least they'll have that message from trusted adults to hang on to.

Boys Will Be Boys

One of the greatest disservices adults do is tolerate obnoxious behavior from boys as simply "boy behavior." Parents of strong moral boys will tell you that's not OK in their house. But this idea that "boys will be boys" and there's nothing wrong with that, or nothing we can do about it, pervades contemporary US society.

Society is shifting somewhat. Suddenly men are realizing their *daughters* are facing an uphill battle against boys who get away with a lot. These fathers of daughters are speaking up.

The highly publicized trial of a star athlete from a prestigious university highlights the shift that is happening. Despite being convicted of multiple sexual assault felonies, largely based on compelling *eyewitness* testimony, the defendant was given a ridiculously short sentence by a lenient judge. Public outcry was so strong that a public effort was launched to remove the judge from future sexual abuse hearings or to remove him altogether. This response would have been unthinkable a decade ago. The courts are slow to catch up, unfortunately. Two other similar cases involving white athletes in the following months yielded similarly brief sentences, with much the same reasons given by the judges. But the tide is turning. Our girls, and our boys, need something better than having obnoxious behavior brushed off rather than addressed.

12

The Hard Stuff

Being open about life's difficult issues

What is it about kids that can get us so tongue-tied over the hard stuff? As parents, we tend to shy away from talking about difficult things with our kids. Even teachers can find it difficult to bring up sensitive, painful, or just plain embarrassing topics in their classrooms. Sex ed class, anyone? I know that my classmates weren't the only ones who found it awkward; my teachers were not super comfortable with it either!

A quote from hockey great Wayne Gretzky is a good life guide here: "You miss 100 percent of the shots you don't take."

So while it's hard to open up the space to talk about hard stuff, it's important to the kids in our life that we do. How we do it matters, of course. What is it kids hear? What space do we hold for them to have and ask questions?

Especially when you're owning your own mistakes, keeping your promises, or talking about difficult topics like sex, death or divorce, it's worth asking yourself this question beforehand: **What do I want to be teaching in this moment?**

Apologizing

When my son was fourteen, a neighbor whose son was about to

turn four asked me, "Your son is so good. Mine is so stubborn. How do you do it?"

Rather than feeling delighted I instantly felt really chastened. A mere two hours before this lovely compliment, I had blown it big-time with my son. Really blown it, swearing included.

So I chose to be honest with her: "Well, if you blow it like I did just a while ago, you go and admit it, apologize, and try to make amends."

I think she was surprised. But she listened.

You might recall I said earlier that I tell my students about this: kids can take you to anger you wouldn't have thought possible for yourself. It's human. Not good, but very human. And this isn't just true of parents, by the way. Anyone who spends extended time with children can find themselves at their limit. Plenty of teachers lose their cool with kids. Typically, teachers can keep themselves from swearing, but even good teachers may speak to kids in ways that are really disrespectful and damaging.

The thing is, when you do screw up in how you talk to a kid, you have choices about what you say and what it teaches them. Here are some things to keep in mind:

1. No child deserves to be yelled at.

I mean this. Even if they've been annoying, frustrating, insulting, demeaning, or downright stupid. Yelling, swearing, or degrading them is not an option.

That means if you do lose your cool, *you*—not they—are in the wrong. That's a hard one for most of us. It seems like admitting that we are in the wrong will detract from our authority. But here's the deal: if you have your authority by yelling, it's not real anyway. It's temporary. An illusion until they are out of your sight or out of your house. And then it's gone.

Authority requires respect. Not fear, but respect. **So when you do lose your cool** (and I'm going to go out on a limb here and say that almost all of us will), **it's what you do *after* that really matters.**

2. Children need to hear us control ourselves.

When I've needed to, I've gone to my kids to apologize. This has to be a private thing, just between the two of you. I've explained that:

1. They didn't deserve to be yelled at.

2. When _____ happened, I felt _____. And it made me lose my temper.

3. I shouldn't have done that, and I am very sorry. I'm sure it felt awful.

4. I'd like to know what I can do to help them feel better, or get us back to what we were doing, or whatever is needed.

Where do you think kids get their understanding of emotions and emotion control? Certainly, from watching us. But since they *are* children, they have incomplete interpretation of what they see. They need our words to help them fully process what is going on around them. Heightened emotion in adults is intense and frightening to young children, and it can be overwhelming or confusing to older ones. They don't like seeing the big people out of control. It draws into question the whole of their reality and how safe that might (or might not) be.

The language we use around how we feel and what that looks like is going to be the language they use to form their understanding. If they see you blow up, they know that adults can do that. If they hear you explain that you see what caused it, that you have it under control, and that you want to help make things better, the whole thing becomes less fearful.

They also need to hear that it wasn't their fault. That they are not to blame. Children will assume that they are, and it is damaging. When adults take responsibility for their own emotions and actions, it frees children to breathe and also to practice that kind of self-control for themselves.

My son, intense and stubborn at times, was already able at the age of twelve to remove himself from a situation that he knew was making him too heated. That's an amazing skill to build. He was also able to recognize when he crossed a line and to come back after he had cooled off to offer a sincere and genuine apology for it, along with ideas for how to handle himself differently in the future. That's pretty awesome. The standard child development literature refers to that as *emotion self-regulation*. I call it being a good person.

Things to Try

1. Think of a time recently when you yelled at or berated a child and about how the child reacted. How could following step 2 above help in a situation like that?

2. The next time you yell or snap at a child, try apologizing afterward. Let the child know that you made a mistake. See what that leads them to do or say.

3. After you've gone through this process a few times, check in to see how you feel about your parenting or teaching. What shifts have happened inside you? How has it impacted your relationships with the children in your life?

Keep Your Promises

I realized it was important for kids to be able to trust what I told them back when my niece Chloe was a baby. My sister, her husband, and new baby moved in with our mom, our mom's mother, and me. We became a four-generation household full of women who were related. My poor brother-in-law!

I spent a year with my baby niece. Chloe is why I became interested in kids, in fact. I was drawn to how cute she was, of course. But especially to how rapidly she changed. She fascinated me. I took my responsibility to her very seriously.

Long before I was out of college, or working in education, it became clear to me that my niece was absorbing everything I said. I started being careful with my words even then. It became important to me that she know that when I said something, I meant it. If I told her I would do something, I would do it. I maintained this just as strongly with her brother when he was born and then with my own kids many years after that.

Keeping my promises doesn't just benefit my kids. It helps me, in the long run. Sticking to what you say and keeping your promises spills into disciplining too; if I say something is going to happen, it will. The kids know this. So it helps with maintaining limits and it helps with explanations.

I'm not alone in this. My friend Laura told me about her friend Julia, who was a highly in-demand nanny before becoming a preschool teacher. Julia was referred to a family who had had it with their kids. They just couldn't deal with them anymore. The friend who referred Julia told them she could help, but they would just need to give her some time. They suggested not to pressure her because what Julia would do would work.

A few weeks into the job, Julia was talking to Laura, and over a cup of tea, a satisfied smile spread across Julia's face. "It happened today."

Laura was puzzled, and asked, "What did?"

"Jake told me, 'I hate you, Julia.'"

What had made her so happy though, was what young Jake had added next: "I hate that you don't lie. If you say something, you mean it and I can't do anything to change it."

Keep in mind that we are always teaching kids, in every interaction. Take a moment to be curious about this. What are your promises, kept and unkept, teaching them about who you are?

Be somebody kids can count on.

Things to Try

1. Notice when you promise children that things will happen. Notice whether you follow through or not.

2. The next time you're about to promise children that something will happen, consciously check that it is something you are committed to making happen.

3. If you realize there was something you said you would do and that it hasn't happened, use it as an opportunity to talk to your kids. Say you realize that you said it and haven't done it yet. Try asking what they think of that or if it's still important for them that it does happen.

Being Open About Difficult Things

I am always frustrated by parents who tell their kids what they think their child wants to hear. Or who lie to supposedly soften the blow. I understand the desire to make our kids' lives the best we can. This can lead people to want to shield their kids from anything uncomfortable. But if something bad is going to happen, what good can it possibly do to lie to kids about it? Whose benefit is that for, exactly?

So here's (yet) another place where my peers thought I was nuts. When my kids were about to get a shot at the doctor's office, they were scared it was going to hurt. Heck, many adults are scared that a shot will hurt! So I wanted to reassure them and also give them a way to prepare and cope. I told my children, "Yes, it's going to hurt, but only for a moment and the nurse will have an ice pack for you." They weren't happy to hear it would hurt, but they braced themselves and got through it with no fuss. They understood what was coming and that they could make it.

If you tell the child a shot's not going to hurt, and then it does, please ask yourself—what do you think the child thinks of you? How likely are they to trust what you say in the future?

Leveling with kids is all about trust, and respect.

Let's tackle *respect* first. I think kids deserve to be leveled with. They're stronger than we think they are, and when they know what's coming, it gives them more to work with. You may not realize this, but kids know when adults are patronizing them or treating them like babies. And they don't like it. I'm not saying to treat them like an adult or as an equal partner. But treating kids with respect is a basic starting point for me.

Being treated with respect builds *trust*. Kids who know that you're going to level with them will trust what you say. They're more willing to work with you. They'll cut you more slack, and they'll tend to appreciate your efforts even when you annoy the heck out of them. (Sorry, thinking of my teens here.)

So what are some of the most difficult things parents or teachers face talking to kids about? I want to take a look with you at the biggies: Sex and Reproduction, Death, Marital Problems, and Catastrophes.

1. Sex and Reproduction

This one is a stumper for a lot of parents. What do you say? And when? Even for teachers this can be a tricky topic.

Sex education seems to be enjoying a bit of a resurgence these days. There are terrific resources online and a brand new children's book that absolutely rocks in terms of speaking openly to kids, *Tell Me About Sex, Grandma*—the latest in Anastasia Higginbotham's wonderful series, *Ordinary Terrible Things*.

I was incredibly lucky on this one. When my kids were little, I had another class parent to lean on and learn from. An OB/GYN, she was invited to visit the kids' classes to talk in age appropriate ways about sex and reproduction. The first time was my daughter's kindergarten year.

Unlike many of us, this mom who delivers babies for a living was incredibly comfortable with the human body and human sexuality! She had a great conversation with the kids, and gave us parents great resources for talking about sex with our kids.

Now, I *really* love doing research! I dig right in, informing myself and learning whatever I can. I grabbed several books. I had already been using anatomical terms rather than baby terms with our kids, like *penis* instead of *peepee*. I already knew I needed to think about sexuality and how to talk about it. It wasn't easy for me though. It wasn't something my own family talked about. Ever. I'm not terribly comfortable with it even now.

So I dove in to the resource list. I read a lot. And I quickly realized I needed to up my game.

My husband and I began to tell our kids honest, factually correct information about human reproduction. We chose to do it as they asked questions, so that it emerged on their timeline and not ours. Each question was answered on the simplest surface level possible, and if the kids had more questions, we added more detail or complexity until they understood at a level that satisfied them. That worked well in the weeks and months after the classroom talk.

Then, about a year later, when our daughter was six and our son was four, I found myself explaining the whole process of intercourse—*waaaay* before I'd expected to.

After a series of increasingly specific explanations, they both kept asking the same question: "Yes, but how does the sperm get to the egg?" They were mystified, curious, and utterly unsatisfied with the answers I'd constructed that left out that one crucial detail.

So I told them.

They were surprised.

Then we had to have another conversation. About how this was private information and they couldn't share it at school. About how they had gotten to hear it from their parents, and their friends deserved the same chance. About how if they shared what they now knew, then their friends wouldn't have that opportunity. Which they both understood. And as far as I know, they both honored it.

So you might wonder, given that they had the whole "talk" that early, were we done? Hardly! As kids develop, their understanding changes. New questions emerge, and old ideas get rewritten. We've revisited that talk in the years that followed.

I got kids' book about bodies and sex and left them lying out for my two kids to access on their own time. The books would sit on the coffee table untouched for months. Then they'd end up in one of the kids' bedrooms, with the door closed. One of the books was a perennial hit in the car (had to be careful with carpools though!).

There are many, many wonderful resources for talking to your kids about sex. There's a cottage industry of people now reaching parents about how to do it well. I put a list of some of our go-to books at the end of this book.

What to Convey about Sex

As happy as I am with how I handled my kids' early years, I've been troubled to see that in their teens I haven't continued as well as I'd started. Bodies and body changes became regular, normal parts of our conversations. Talking about boundaries flowed easily from there. We talk about consent, sexual assault, and appropriate exploration. But there was a huge gaping hole in what I brought up: pleasure. Even intimacy. I was blind to the fact that in all our conversations, sex came to be about reproduction or threat.

Then recently, I heard a sexual health educator who inspired me. Her name is Marnie Goldenberg, and her blog is called *sexplainer*. Her message—that sex is a positive force for good in the world—was exactly what I needed to hear. It's not so far removed from what I'd said to the kids when they were little, but the framing is different, and it's vitally important. Here, at last, was the positive message I'd been lacking—the message that sex extends beyond the reproductive aspects and risk aspects—to allow room for talking about intimacy and pleasure.

Hearing Goldenberg brought into sharp relief what I had left out. Her message is so joyful and so positive. Her strong belief is that kids need to hear that sex is a positive force in life, early, from their parents, *before* they inevitably learn that some people use it to hurt others. It makes so much sense.

This book is offered as an opportunity, rather than a burden. I hope veteran parents and teachers will read it without feeling guilty about what they could have done. Hearing Marnie Goldenberg's message was my moment for this in my own parenting. I wish I had known this when my kids were little. I wish I could have done a better job for them than the one I've done. And I can't. I'm what I call sad/happy—letting go of what I didn't do and the lost time behind us, even as I'm excited to open up to a new road ahead. So I'm grabbing the moment right now to show them what I've just learned and to offer up the next, better version of my parenting.

2. Death

How do you talk to children about death? When should you start? I found out when our daughter was five.

Our daughter started kindergarten at a small school with a close, supportive community. A couple months into the school year, something unthinkable happened. A child who had been in the junior kindergarten class the year before, but who no longer attended the school, died from illness. It was sudden and truly horrific. While we were saddened, our new friends and classmates who had spent the previous school year with the family were devastated.

Prior to that, I hadn't even contemplated what to say to my children about death. The principal, January Handl, was a gifted parent educator with particular expertise in dealing with death. She worked with each class to help kids process the death in age-appropriate ways. She also worked with the parents, offering ideas and resources. I devoured them. I came away greatly changed.

I learned in all the reading and all the conversations that **children *must* be dealt with directly about death.** Our U.S. society has shied away from it. Like me, most parents never even think about it, or about what to say. We were fortunate, in that we didn't know the family and so our experience of their loss was easier to bear. But the exposure forever changed my parenting.

I began having conversations with my children that included the topic and concepts of death whenever they were relevant. I recall very clearly a conversation that took place at a coffeeshop near our house. We were talking about animals, when my son, then four, said, "And then they'll die some day." The conversations around us came to an abrupt stop, and I felt many eyes turn our way. Every parent knows this feeling—when whatever you are about to do/say is on public display. It's uncomfortable. Plus, I knew I had an opportunity to normalize death for my son.

I looked at my son and as straightforwardly as I could said, "Yes, they will. All things die eventually."

He went on, "What happens to their bodies?"

So I explained, simply—and surprising even to myself—quite comfortably about burials and decomposition. He was fascinated. Not in a gory or sensationalist way, but in a genuine, respectful, and curious way. He came away satisfied, and the topic shifted naturally to another interest.

Kids really can handle more than people give them credit for. That said, there are also limits to what young children can actually fully understand.

Kids' Understanding of Death

My experience led me to cover the understanding of death in my child development classes. In coming to terms with death, the main conceptual piece for children to understand is its permanence. Unlike in the movies when someone is killed and then comes back to life, people don't work that way. Death really is final. That's a hard one for young children to wrap their heads around.

Death has four aspects that kids gradually come to understand across childhood.

Aspects of death	Kids can understand by
It's final	about age 5
It's inevitable	about age 5
It's not just for old people	about age 9
It's irreversible	about age 10

Researchers find that kids don't fully comprehend death as a whole package until about age ten. That may sound old to you, but there's a lot to figure out about death. Obviously, children's understanding is influenced by whether they have had personal experiences. It's also influenced very highly by what they're told.

Unlike adults who basically "get it" when someone dies, children actually have to spend time and energy figuring out what has happened. They are piecing together their understanding, and our words are very powerful at these times.

In fact, even when we have good intentions, kids may seriously misunderstand what we say.

My friend Nikki saw this firsthand. Nikki's niece was just seven when her mother died. Well-meaning friends of the family wanted to reassure the child. They told her lovingly, "It's OK. Your mother was so good. She's gone to Heaven."

In the coming days and weeks, the little girl's behavior changed dramatically. That's very common as children grapple with making sense of a death. The problem is that the girl was acting out at home and in school, fighting and causing trouble. She was, Nikki told me, wholly unlike the sweet child she usually was. Finally, Nikki took her aside and asked what was up. No one else had asked! The little girl explained very plainly, "I don't want to die. If you're good, you die and go to Heaven."

This poor little grieving child was determined to do what she needed to do to keep living! Thankfully, Nikki was able to clear up the confusion, and her niece eased back to her own sweet self.

Too often, adults want to soften the blow for kids, or they hope to protect them from the harsh reality of life. I am hopeful that this story, and others I share later about my own children, can help dispel the feeling that sheltering children is necessary, or even a good idea. Kids need to be leveled with.

Phrases to Avoid

First, let's look at some common phrases people use, to talk about death, and why they're unhelpful to children:

"She's sleeping now." Young children can easily freak out at bedtime after hearing this. They have no way of reconciling the sleeping they do every night with this metaphor. Rather than consoling or softening, this can really backfire.

"He's gone away." Young children make sense of this and figure he'll be back sometime. They'll keep asking, which is usually upsetting to the adults, and confusing to the child. It leaves the death unsettled, unresolved, and unclear.

"She's gone to a better place." Kids just wonder where the heck that is and why they can't go visit—especially if it's so nice there!

What to Say Instead

Instead, parents, teachers, and other caring **adults should talk to kids in real terms about death.** Give kids the space and support to process their feelings, and to ask questions or talk about whatever they're thinking.

These may sound cold to you, but here are examples of simple and straightforward acknowledgements of death that allow for the conversation to *open*, not stop:

- "She died."
- "Yes, he is dead now."
- "Her body doesn't work anymore."

What about God, or Heaven? If they are part of your family's belief, then of course you want to talk to your children about them. I'm absolutely not saying to leave them out. What I'm saying is that it's important to give children language for what happens to the person's body, since that's the thing they are accustomed to seeing and that's what they can understand.

It would also really help kids a great deal if the adults in their lives could help them build a more complete and normalized view of death.

The thing to keep in mind is that movies, television, and other media are telling kids a great deal—much of it confusing or oversimplified. Completely separate from whether a child's family holds religious beliefs or not, it is possible to talk about death as a natural and inevitable part of life without scarring young children. Everything born will die. The surprising thing in society today is this doesn't have to be traumatic for kids to learn.

Attending a Memorial

That first encounter with death when our daughter was five turned out to be good training. Three years later, I lost one of my dearest friends to a catastrophic stroke, at the age of thirty-five. Deb left behind a loving husband and a gorgeous three-year-old whom my children adored. Our whole network of friends was in shock. I allowed my children, then eight and six, to see me grieve in full. I attended the funeral without them, but our family attended the memorial service.

I talked to them beforehand about her death and what the memorial service would be like. I tried to give them some idea of what to expect and a way of describing what was going on. We talked about how I felt—how sad I was and how hard it was to have to say good-bye to my friend. We talked about what would happen to her body. We talked a lot about her little girl and how she would feel and cope.

As it turned out, lots of children attended the memorial. It was truly a celebration of Deb's life, and a wonderful opportunity for my kids to see death as a normal part of life. It also reinforced for them the value of community.

Attending a Burial

Two years later, my son's friend and classmate Dylan lost his father to cancer. My kids went to a very small school, one class per grade, where the kids and families got to know each other very well. The family was incredibly open about the dad's illness, sharing his progress and process of dying. It was an incredible gift to the community. Throughout the year, we talked at home about what came up at school and how the family was doing.

After Rick's death, I felt it was incredibly important that we attend not just the memorial, but the funeral and burial as well, in support of Kimberly and their boys. I'm so glad we did. It gave our children, then ten and eight, the opportunity to see up close both profound grief and glorious coping. Again, we talked beforehand about what might take place. I think it really helps to prepare kids with some idea of what they will experience. We talked about how Dylan, and his mom and brother, were feeling, and also how my son was feeling. Like most kids his age, he was sad for his friend, but he didn't really have deep feelings about the father himself. He could have felt odd about saying that, but there was no need. We opened the door for him to talk, and he let us know what he was thinking.

We were one of only two families who brought their children to the burial. It was a profound experience: kids laughing and playing, and parents coming together in grief and support of Kimberly and the boys. It felt right. Rick's two young sons were surviving their loss. They and life would continue.

Dying

When our kids were not quite twelve and ten I got completely unexpected news that my mother's breast cancer had returned with a vengeance. Stage 4, in her bones and liver. I chose to be open with them at every step—not alarmist, but open. We talked about her illness and her treatments, however, at the beginning, I didn't introduce that the disease would kill her. None of us could know at that point how long she might actually have, and thinking about that seemed more of a burden than a help. We were very frank about how grave it was, though, and how hard the treatments were on her. We talked with the kids about the complications my mom faced and the medical procedures she underwent.

Two years in to her treatments, my mom came to live with us for several months. By this point we were open with the kids about the disease being fatal, yet also clear that there was no way to know how long she would have. She was determined to stick around and handled the chemotherapy very well. Our kids were unfazed by her lack of hair, or her puffiness, or any of it. They recognized these as side effects and simply looked beyond them. They took their grandmother as they always had and loved having the time with her. Returning my mom to Georgia at the end of that visit was one of the hardest things I've ever done. I was open with the kids that living three thousand miles away, I didn't know if we would see her again. But despite an initial prediction from her oncologist of around six months, we were blessed with almost three years.

My mother's funeral was without question the hardest one I've done with my kids. I don't know how I would have coped with my own grief and also made room for theirs, if we hadn't worked up to it.

3. Marital Problems Like Money and Divorce

Half of all marriages in the United States end in divorce. Even those that don't, experience low points and tension. So it's without question that parents and families will argue from time to time. Yet most of us feel that we can't acknowledge this to our kids—that keeping it unspoken will somehow protect them, or possibly us.

It turns out it's incredibly important to level with children, *especially* about difficult things happening in the home. In his illuminating book *Kids Pick up on Everything*, David Code presents evidence from studies in medicine, psychology, and neuroscience to support the idea that when parents are stressed, kids do pick up on it and, in fact, suffer. He details the illnesses (like asthma and type I diabetes) and mental health conditions (including ADHD and schizophrenia) that have been shown to increase in families when the parents are stressed. Code walks a careful line between identifying parent stress as a source of child ailment and yet not blaming parents. He talks extensively about the changes to society that have led to greater isolation and hence increased stress. He offers strategies for decreasing stress, primarily focused on relaxing and connecting with people more.

The underlying point in Code's work is that regardless of its cause, parent stress is bad for kids because they pick up on it and it impacts them negatively.

Other research backs this up. Longitudinal studies, such as work by psychologist Mavis Hetherington and sociologist Yongmin Sun, suggest that the biggest negative impact of divorce comes leading up to it, not afterward (e.g, Hetherington & Elmore, 2003; Hetherington & Kelly, 2003; Sun & Li, 2008, 2009). We need to keep in mind that the tension and instability in the home resulting in divorce may be what causes kids the most difficulty.

Being open with kids is a vital way of diffusing that tension.

Sociologist Paul Amato has been studying divorce in the United States for almost twenty years (e.g., Amato, 2010). He has found that factors affecting how kids cope with divorce well are *active* coping skills, like seeking peer connections or help from counselors. Factors that get in kids' way of rebounding after a divorce are *avoidant* coping skills, often including blaming themselves or feeling little or no control. Being open with kids is the necessary first step to helping them develop active coping skills.

Since children and teens are picking up on the tension anyway, it helps to give them the words and explanations to understand it better or more fully. Here again, our words have the power to shape what kids think and feel. Being honest with them about family struggles or financial difficulties serves many purposes:

1. *It gives them the security of knowing that it's not them.* All children, even teens, will assume to some extent that when the adults in their lives are unhappy, they are somehow the cause of it. Talking to children openly about conflict gives them a way of being certain that they are not to blame.

2. *It shows them the respect that talking to them signifies—especially for teens.* Far better to deal with a known problem than the imagined ones. As I said earlier, kids can handle much more than we credit them with. Teens, especially, need to be leveled with. They are building their capacity for living an independent adult life. Conversations about difficulties the family faces will help prepare them for that. They may face the same problem later in life, in which case knowing more now will help. They will certainly face other difficulties. Knowing more about how the adults in their life cope, address, and face difficulties will give children tools to work with.

3. *It fights off learned helplessness and the increasing anxiety that comes with it.* Both Code and Martin Seligman address this in their work (e.g., see Seligman's book *Flourish*). Remember, kids *are* picking up on it. But if it stays "hidden," or behind closed doors, there's nothing children can do to help themselves feel better. Learned helplessness is the state that develops when a person believes that no matter their actions, bad things will

happen. It's a terrible, demotivating, at times debilitating, state to live in. It disempowers people because at their core, they believe that whatever they do, it won't matter.

Our words have everything to do with kids building a sense of learned helplessness or its angelic twin, agency. When we talk to kids about the difficulties we are facing, we can also show them how we are working on them. Our language can help kids/teens build an understanding of what it takes to navigate adult life and that they have the potential capacity to do that too.

4. *It can even bring families closer together.* When parents are fighting, no one in the family feels safe. Talking about it more openly can begin to dissolve that barrier. Parents who are willing to talk to their kids may also find that their kids, in turn, are better able to work with the parent.

5. *If you're following the points in this book, you may even find your kids offer ideas and solutions.*

Elections and World Calamities

Hopefully by now, the point is clear: talking to kids is better than pretending bad stuff isn't happening.

Even the American Academy of Pediatrics is on board with this one. Their website for parents, HealthyChildren.org, offers advice on how to address real-world issues with children of all ages. In their Emotional Wellness section, an article on talking to children about disasters opens with this statement: "Children can cope more effectively with a disaster when they feel they understand what is happening and what they can do to help protect themselves, family, and friends. Provide basic information to help them understand, without providing unnecessary details that may only alarm them."

And therein lies the real challenge for parents. What's necessary and what is too much? What will alarm this child, at this time?

A case in point: the 2016 presidential election resulted in an outcome that stunned the United States and the world. Two simple and incontrovertible facts about the campaign run by President Donald Trump are that:

1. It was brilliantly effective.

2. The anger it unleashed was frightening to children across the country.

Many parents and teachers were at a loss to explain to the children in their lives what would happen in the wake of the election. Newsletters, websites, and the news media were filled with stories about how teachers could and did respond. One *Huffington Post* article, "What Do We Tell the Children?," advised right up front: "Tell them, first, that we will protect them."

The author, Ali Michael, PhD, opened the article this way: "Tell them, first, that we will protect them. Tell them that we have democratic processes in the U.S. that make it impossible for one mean person to do too much damage. Tell them that we will protect those democratic processes—and we will use them—so that Trump is unable to act on many of the false promises he made during his campaign." I respectfully disagree, from a child development perspective.

The thing is—and this is hard to read and hard to take—we can't guarantee that we *will* be able to protect kids. On the first day following the election, there were three verified cases of young women in hijab being grabbed and attacked on college campuses. Were their parents or teachers able to keep them safe? We won't be with our children 24/7. We don't have control over what the crazies may do. We don't know when an insane gunman might come to their school. In fact, parents and teachers often don't even know about bullying that happens right under their noses.

It does more harm than good to tell children we will protect them and then fall short. So what can we do?

I agree with one point: reassure them. Just don't overpromise. In the wake of catastrophes and upheaval, offer a calm presence, tell children the simplest version of the facts, and point out what is being done to help. Then wait for them to ask for more.

Things to Try

1. Listen for hard places that come up. Notice how you feel about them. Do you instinctively hedge or try to shield the children in your life?

2. If you feel it's completely beyond you, notice that. Be accepting of the feeling and then dive into learning more so that you become more able to have these conversations with kids. (I list some resources at the end of the book.)

3. Look for places that present themselves as opportunities to open up small starter conversations on difficult topics like death or sex. Make small steps at first, just mentioning the ideas.

Open and Supportive

It is, of course, possible to be open but not terribly helpful.

On a family trip in Queensland, Australia, when I was eight years old, we had a chance to go into a rainforest. My sister squealed that there would be leeches and refused to go in. She preferred to wait at the car (with, I might add, our mother). I looked at my dad, a research scientist whom I trusted to know about these things. I was dying to see the rainforest. I wanted reassurance. Instead, I got fact: "It's a rainforest Muffie. Of course there will be leeches."

I didn't go in.

I still regret it. I regretted it as soon as I saw my brother's back disappear into the thick green foliage. I regretted it the entire time I was stuck in the car with my mom and sister, missing out on seeing and walking through a real live rainforest. When my brother and father returned with their legs *covered* in leeches, I admit I did have a brief moment of respite from that regret. But once they had removed them (which turned out not only to be easy, but actually pretty fascinating), the regret returned hard.

I've said kids need to be leveled with. And yet, that doesn't mean just be blunt. They need the truth, but not always the whole truth. They need the truth, but sometimes to have it softened. They need the truth, and also the tools to face it.

Go back to the example from the doctor's office. I told my kids, "Yes, it's going to hurt, but only for a moment and the nurse will have an ice pack for you."

I could have just said, "It's a shot. Of course it's going to hurt."

That would have been true but not ultimately helpful. Instead, I leveled with them about the pain, *and* I also minimized the need to worry about it. I gave them a way to put it into context (it would hurt only briefly) and told them about the help they would receive (the ice pack from the nurse). The kids sat for their shots like little troopers.

My children knew what was going to happen. They trusted what I was saying. And they believed they were ready to handle it well.

That is what we're shooting for, yes?

Things to Try

1. Look for the next time when you need to deliver uncomfortable news to a child. Notice if you have any hesitation or discomfort.

2. When a topic comes up that is hard to talk about or is potentially frightening to a child, ask yourself first what aspects of it the child needs to know about and how you can deliver those pieces along with an idea for coping with it.

3. Be kind to yourself as you stretch into this new, hard terrain. It helps to remember that you are learning, too.

13

The Bottom Line

How we speak matters too

Hopefully, I've been able to show you many ways in which what we say to children shapes what they think.

It also matters *how* we speak to them. I'd like to offer four lessons for us all to keep in mind as we work with children.

Use Your Words Wisely

The idea that we should speak with care is certainly not new. Many traditions, especially religious or spiritual ones, include this notion at their foundation.

In his lovely book *The Four Agreements*, don Miguel Ruiz explores the knowledge of the ancient Toltec people, whom most of us know nothing about. He identifies the Toltec as a society whose purpose was to understand and preserve spiritual wisdom from even more ancient people. Despite its unfamiliarity and ancient origins, when Oprah included the book in her Book Club, sales soared to over five million copies. The book resonates with many who read it.

Ruiz introduces the concept "Be impeccable with your word" as the first agreement, calling it "the most important one and also the most difficult one to honor" (1997, 25). He goes on to say " Your word is the power that you have to create" and "the word is a force" (1997, 26).

The Buddhist concept of *right speech* is another example. The Dalai Lama is often paraphrased as saying if it is not necessary and kind, don't say it. At its simplest, right speech is about speaking compassionately. At a deeper level, the idea is at the core of Buddhist philosophy, one of the principal components referred to as the eight-fold path. The eight are a complete guide for better, more moral living.

In schools across the United States, the idea of right speech has been lifted and sanitized of its religious flavor and turned into a tool for students. Curriculum guides and motivational posters with acronym reminders like "THINK before you speak" abound. Students are taught and reminded that their words should be True, Helpful, Inspiring, Necessary, and Kind. Actually, there are many versions of what THINK stands for. The THI move around quite a bit, but most seem to agree on Necessary and Kind. (If you want to see what I'm talking about, check Google images for "THINK poster.")

It seems pretty straightforward that kids need to learn to be civil with others. The idea of compassion is trickier for a lot of people in the United States. It is starting to get more press, though, and like mindfulness, is entering the mainstream rapidly. Until recently, compassion was mischaracterized as weak, wimpy, or something only women offer to others. As research into compassion explodes, the findings are being popularized. People's notions of what compassion means and what it requires are changing.

I'm not advocating that schools should teach children compassion (that's a separate issue for another day). I am saying, though, that we need to teach them to speak both civilly and with care.

So what do we say to children to help them develop this capacity?

It starts—as all steps do—with the words we ourselves use. Each of us is called to "be impeccable" with our words, as don Miguel Ruiz suggests. To speak clearly and kindly. That means no raging at the driver who cuts you off on the freeway. No smack talking about the woman in line ahead of you in the grocery store. No snide comments about someone else's child or about that child's parent.

There's a meme that I see shared often by friends I admire: "You can tell who the strong women are. They're the ones building each other up instead of tearing each other down."

When we use our words to lift others up, our children learn that words are a positive force in the world. That's what don Miguel Ruiz was referring to when he said, "the word is a force." It can be positive or it can be negative. It's up to us. And since we have a choice, every time we open our mouths, we need to choose wisely. Children absorb all that we say and the implications behind the words as well.

Pattern or Possibility?

A spiritual teacher I follow online offers this clarifying perspective: Do you see people as Pattern or as Possibility?

Much of this book calls us to be open—to the child in front of us and to our own reactions and preconceptions. It can be difficult to maintain an open, positive frame in the whirl of household life or classroom chaos.

It helps to realize that what we expect shapes what we say. As we saw in the story about the math teacher who had hidden beliefs about girls needing to work harder than boys to do as well as them, she didn't know she held those beliefs. She was able to hear her own words, though, and was brave enough and strong enough to examine them honestly.

Being with children calls us to be our best selves. They require it. They deserve it. These little humans who have not been on the planet as long as we have are learning from us at all times. As the meme goes, be the person your dog thinks you are. So that you can be that person for your kids too.

Ultimately, Not Talking but Listening

Our words shape what kids think and feel. Our silences do too.

When we take the time to listen to kids, they open up. By listening to children we signal to them that they are worth our time. That their ideas and feelings matter to us. That *they* matter to us. This is incredibly important to a child's development.

I have a friend whose experience is a lot like many other immigrant children's. Joan's Asian parents found that when she acted like a regular US teenager, their worldview was dishonored. This is a common experience in immigrant families, and one which my students spoke of often. As the child grows up in two worlds, the rules governing behavior in those worlds can contradict each other—resulting in conflicts and fights. I've had many undergraduate students tell me their parents wouldn't support them through high school. Several were told by parents to move out. In Joan's case, it literally resulted in her father not speaking to her for several years—even while they lived in the same house.

This problem isn't unique to immigrant parents of course. Many parents dictate to their children, believing it is for their own good. Teachers, too, fall prey to this belief. What is the message kids get though? That they are worthwhile? Or ... ?

I'm not saying that whatever kids do is fine. There are clearly many examples of when it is not. But we do need to listen to them. And establishing a relationship in which you *can* listen and they can genuinely share their thoughts takes time. It starts with being careful with your words, and understanding that what you say will shape what kids believe.

A Spiritual Enterprise

I'd like to close with one more thought. What I'm about to say here has no bearing on the research or classroom examples presented in the rest of the book, and it does not reflect the views of the researchers who did that work. I know nothing about the religious perspectives of the people whose stories I've shared here.

This section changes none of what I've written. If it does anything at all, it only deepens the meaning of what you've already read.

To me, raising children is a spiritual enterprise. It doesn't matter if they are your children or not. If you are a person in a child's life, that is a kind of sacred responsibility. Children aren't just short humans who have spent less time on the planet. They are portals into our souls.

We are called to be better people when we are caring for a child. Putting a child's needs ahead of our own is, in my opinion, one of the things that completes us as people. This has nothing to do with biological reproduction. It has to do with having a child in your life whom you care deeply about. Anyone can experience this transformation.

What it takes is selflessness. What it takes is recognizing the need of someone else—this child—and setting aside your own needs as the primary driver of your life. We grow up when we do this. We mature. And, I believe, in doing this, we step closer to the source of all life. Call it love, call it God, call it whatever you like. Children bring us to this place of recognition that we are not the most important thing in the world.

That's not to say this is easy work.

When working with children, I've found these three reminders helpful:

- Abide—sit with life as it is, in this moment, and live into it fully.
- Surrender—to the wisdom of something bigger than any of us.
- Accept—the responsibility of moving toward our best self.

We do not need to be perfect at what we're doing. We just need to be caring, committed, and open to learning along the way.

I hope this book will bring you joy, discomfort, answers, and more questions. I hope it will illuminate something useful in your life that you can bring to your interactions with children. I hope it has made you smile, and ponder, and think. I thank you for the time you have taken to read it. May the good that arises from these words go out into the world for the well-being of children everywhere.

Acknowledgments

What a year it has been writing this book! I have so much to be thankful for and so many people to thank for helping me reach this point.

I am grateful first and foremost for the spaces that exist for me to write in—I can't get a word written at home! Without these vital, welcoming, community-filled places, this book would never have happened. Thank you to the wonderful folks at Breathe Together's Mandala Tea House, Snake & Butterfly Chocolate Factory, and my local Peet's Coffee.

From the very first day of committing to writing, I have talked to anyone and everyone about what I'm doing. The universe has returned nothing but good wishes and support. To everyone whose ear I've talked off, thank you for listening and helping me hone my message about this book. To each of you who has provided ideas, suggestions, contacts, and encouragement, I thank you from the bottom of my heart. Taking the leap to write has been a huge risk, and I have needed every word of your help.

I am grateful to the friends who are writers for teaching me about this process. To Allen Collins, for your time and perspective as I launched into this. To Sybil Lockhart, for assuring me at the very start that if what I have to say wants out this badly, it is worth writing. To Mindy Pelz-Hall, for sharing what you've learned about self-publishing and for leading me to my editor, Jennifer Read Hawthorne. To Jennifer, for introducing me to the editing process and for ensuring I can release this book with the confidence that I'm offering my best work.

I have learned so much from so many masterful educators. Thank you to the colleagues and classroom teachers—especially the phenomenal educators at Children's Center for the Stanford Community, Mulberry School, and Discovery Charter School—whose wisdom is included here. I am so very grateful for your tutelage.

Thank you to the many friends who lent their stories. Being able to include your voice and life lessons enriches this book tremendously.

I am grateful to the family and friends who have encouraged me, even when they thought this was crazy.

To the Jens at Breathe Together, your early and ongoing support has held the space for me to lean into my fear and do this work.

To my sister, Lisa, who has been one of my all-time champions, cheering me on at every point.

To my daughter, Eva, for your deeply held belief in me.

To my son, Oscar, for your unwavering enthusiasm for this new path I'm taking.

To my husband, Scott, for holding the space for me to do this and for reading, commenting, reviewing, and loving me through this.

Thank you all.

May I bring the joy and love I've received during this project out into the world to do more good.

Resources for Difficult Topics

Death

Books for kids:

Children's literature is full of great books (many written long ago) that help kids face and work through the experience of death.

Charlotte's Web, by E.B. White (1952) is the best example many educators turn to. This story of a pig who is saved by a spider with whom he becomes close friends, offers lessons on love and keeping memories of our loved ones alive even after their death.

The 10ᵗʰ Good Thing about Barney, by Judith Viorst (1971/1987) is my personal favorite. This story of a boy whose beloved cat dies is both tender and straightforward. We found a movie made of it—on videotape—which my cat-loving daughter watched endlessly.

City Dog, Country Frog, by Mo Willems & Jon J. Muth (2010) is another favorite. This lyrically beautiful story of friendship across the seasons only implies the death. It shows how friends teach us to be better people.

For parents I can suggest a couple of starter books:

Talking About Death, by Earl A. Grollman (1990)—a practical guidebook that lays out the kinds of questions kids may have and includes some read-aloud material for young children.

Lifetimes, by Melanie Bryan & Robert Ingpen (1983)—this informative book normalizes death as part of the life cycle of living things. Can be read by a parent and then shared with kids.

Sex Ed

I'm a strong believer in putting resources into kids' hands. And just to be clear—both boys and girls should read all these books. A lot of benefit can come from demystifying the opposite sex! Men who will have female partners in their lives or may later have daughters would do well to understand women's bodies. Same for women who will partner with men or raise sons.

My personal favorites for kids and teens are:

It's Perfectly Normal, by Robie Harris & Michael Emberly (1999/2009). This illustrated book for kids is straightforward and honest in a kid-appropriate way. My kids loved it. The other titles in this series are also great.

Tell Me About Sex, Grandma, by Anastasia Higginbotham (2017). This illustrated book features a grandmother imparting life wisdom that is respectful, honest, and affirming.

The Care and Keeping of You: The Body Book for Girls Book 1 for younger (2012), Book 2 for older (2013), by American Girl. Promotes healthy body awareness.

What's Going on Down There? A Boy's Guide to Growing Up, by Karen Gravelle (1997/2017). Slightly humorous and very direct.

Scarleteen Sex Education for the Real World (scarleteen.com)—a resource-intensive website started by Heather Corinna. Written for older teens and young adults, it also contains great info for parents.

Book from Scarleteen: *S.E.X. The All-You-Need-to-Know Sexuality Guide to Get You Through Your Teens and Twenties* (2007/2016).

For parents and teachers, my go-to sources are the following websites:

talkingaboutsex.com—a website by sexual health educator Anya Manes. She focuses on helping parents have healthy, productive conversations with their children about sex and sexuality.

sexplainer.com—a website by sexual health educator Marnie Goldberg. Factual, candid info about kids and teens, with advice on "helping you raise sexually intelligent kids."

meganmaas.com—the website of Megan Maas, sex researcher and sex educator who specializes in research into pornography and its impact on the development of teens and young adults.

beheroes.net—a website by sex educator/therapist Jo Langford, who writes for teens and parents of teens, but especially boys.

Bibliography

Akhtar, Nameera and Jennifer Menjivar. "Cognitive and Linguistic Correlates of Early Exposure to More Than One Language." *Advances in Child Development and Behavior 42,* (2012): 41-78.

Always. #LikeAGirl. (2014). https://www.youtube.com/watch?v=XjJQBjWYDTs

Amato, Paul R. "Research on Divorce: Continuing Trends and New Developments." *Journal of Marriage and Family* 72, (2010): 650-666.

American Academy of Pediatrics. "Policy Statement: Media and Young Minds." *Pediatrics* 138, no. 5 (Nov 2016). e20162591

—. "Talking to Children About Disasters." Last updated 11/21/2015. https://www.healthychildren.org/English/healthy-living/emotional-wellness/Pages/Talking-to-Children-about-Disasters.aspx

—. "Where We Stand: Screen Time." Last updated 11/01/2016. https://www.healthychildren.org/English/family-life/Media/Pages/Where-We-Stand-TV-Viewing-Time.aspx

Bigler, Rebecca S. and Lynn S. Liben. "A Developmental Intergroup Theory of Social Stereotypes and Prejudice." *Advances in Child Development and Behavior 34,* (2006): 39-89.

Boaler, Jo and Tesha Sengupta-Irving. "Nature, Neglect and Nuance: Changing Accounts of Sex, Gender and Mathematics." In *The SAGE Handbook of Gender and Education,* 207-220. Edited by Christine Skelton and Becky Francis. London: Sage Publications, 2006. http://www.youcubed.org/wp-content/uploads/boaler_senguptainthandbook.pdf

Boaler, Jo. *Experiencing School Mathematics: Traditional and Reform Approaches to Teaching and Their Impact on Student Learning, Revised and Expanded Edition.* Mahwah, NJ: Lawrence Erlbaum, 2002.

Brentari, Diane and Marie Coppola. "What Sign Language Creation Teaches Us About Language." *Wiley Interdisciplinary Reviews (WIRES): Cognitive Science* 4, (2013) 201–211. doi:10.1002/wcs.1212

Brown, Brené. *I Thought it Was Just Me: Women Reclaiming Power and Courage in a Culture of Shame.* New York: Gotham, 2007.

Bruderer, Alison, D. Kyle Danielson, Kandhadai Padmapria, and Janet Werker. "Sensorimotor Influences on Speech Perception in Infancy." *Proceedings of the National Academy of Sciences* 112, no 44 (2015): 13531–13536. doi: 10.1073/pnas.1508631112

Buchsbaum, Daphna, Alison Gopnik, Thomas L. Griffiths, and Patrick Shafto. "Children's Imitation of Causal Action Sequences is Influenced by Statistical and Pedagogical Evidence." *Cognition* 120, no 3 (2011): 331-40. doi:10.1016/j.cognition.2010.12.001

Carey, Susan and Elsa Bartlett. "Acquiring a Single New Word." *Proceedings of the Stanford Child Language Conference* 15, (1978): 17–29.

Cimpian, Joseph R., Sarah T. Lubienski, Jennifer D. Timmer, Martha B. Makowski, and Emily K. Miller. "Have Gender Gaps in Math Closed? Achievement, Teacher Perceptions, and Learning Behaviors Across Two ECLS-K Cohorts." *AERA Open* 2, no. 4 (October 2016). doi: 10.1177/2332858416673617

Code, David. *Kids Pick up on Everything: How Parental Stress is Toxic to Kids.* 2011.

Crowley, Kevin, Maureen Callanan, Harriet Tenenbaum, and Elizabeth Allen. "Parents Explain More Often to Boys than to Girls During Shared Scientific Thinking." *Psychological Science* 12, no. 3 (2001): 258-261.

Dearing, Michael. "Factory vs. Studio." https://medium.com/@mcgd/factory-vs-studio-fb83b3fe9e14

Duckworth, Angela. *Grit: The Power of Passion and Perseverance.* New York: Simon and Schuster, 2016.

Dweck, Carol. *Mindset: The New Psychology of Success.* New York: Ballantine Books, 2006.

Faber, Adele and Elaine Mazlish. *How To Talk So Kids Will Listen & Listen So Kids Will Talk.* New York: Avon Books, 1980/1999.

—. "The Perils of Comparison." In *Siblings Without Rivalry: How To Help Your Children Live Together So You Can Live Too,* 51-66. New York: Harper Collins, 1987/2012.

Fay, Jim and Foster Cline. *Love and Logic.* loveandlogic.com

Fernald, Anne, Virginia A. Marchman and Adriana Weisleder. "SES Differences in Language Processing Skill and Vocabulary are Evident at 18 Months." *Developmental Science* 16, no. 2 (Dec 8 2012): 1-13. doi: 10.1111/desc.12019

Files, Julia A., Anita P. Mayer, Marcia G. Ko, Patricia Friedrich, Marjorie Jenkins, Michael J. Bryan, Suneela Vegunta, et al.

"Speaker Introductions at Internal Medicine Grand Rounds: Forms of Address Reveal Gender Bias." *Journal of Women's Health* 26, no. 5 (2017): 413-419. doi:10.1089/jwh.2016.6044

First People. "Two Wolves: A Cherokee Legend." http://www.firstpeople.us/FP-Html-Legends/TwoWolves-Cherokee.html

Fivush, R., & K. Nelson. "Mother-Child Talk About the Past Locates the Self in Time." *British Journal of Developmental Psychology* 24, (2006): 235 – 251.

Fivush, R., and F.A. Fromhoff. "Style and Structure in Mother-Child Conversations About the Past." *Discourse Processes* 11, (1988): 337–355.

Fivush, R., Haden, C., & Reese, E. "Remembering, Recounting and Reminiscing: The Development of Autobiographical Memory in Social Context." In *Reconstructing our Past: An Overview of Autobiographical Memory,* 341 – 359. Edited by D. Rubin. New York: Cambridge University Press, 1996.

Fivush, Robyn, Catherine Haden and Elaine Reese. "Elaborating on Elaborations: Role of Maternal Reminiscing Style in Cognitive and Socioemotional Development." *Child Development* 77, no. 6 (2006): 1568-1588.

Fredrickson, Barbara. *Positivity.* New York: Crown Publishers, 2009.

Gholipour, Bahar. "The Gender Gap in Math Starts in Kindergarten: And Teachers May be Unknowingly Reinforcing It, a Study Shows." *Huffington Post,* October 27, 2016. http://www.huffingtonpost.com/entry/math-gender-gap-kindergarten_us_581215abe4b064e1b4b0c0a9

Golinkoff, Roberta and Hirsh-Pasek, Kathy. "Introduction: Progress on the Verb Learning Front." In *Action Meets Word: How Children Learn Verbs,* Edited by Kathy Hirsh-Pasek and Roberta Golinkoff. Oxford: Oxford University Press, 2010.

Hanson, Rick and Richard Mendius. *Buddha's Brain: The Practical Neuroscience of Happiness, Love, and Wisdom.* Oakland, CA: New Harbinger, 2009.

Hart, Betty and Todd R. Risley. *Meaningful Differences in the Everyday Experience of Young American Children.* Baltimore, MD: Paul H. Brookes Publishing Company, 1995.

Hetherington, Mavis and Anne Mitchell Elmore. "Risk and Resilience in Children Coping with Their Parents' Divorce and Remarriage." In *Resilience and Vulnerability: Adaptation in the*

Context of Childhood Adversities, 182-212. Edited by Suniya S. Luthar. New York: Cambridge University Press, 2003.

Hetherington, Mavis and John Kelly. *For Better or Worse: Divorce Reconsidered*. New York: W. W. Norton, 2003.

Higginbotham, Anastasia. *Tell Me About Sex, Grandma*. New York: Feminist Press, 2017.

Hilliard, Lacey J. and Lynn S. Liben. "Differing Levels of Gender Salience in Preschool Classrooms: Effects on Children's Gender Attitudes and Intergroup Bias." *Child Development* 81, no. 6 (2010): 1787-98. doi:10.1111/j.1467-8624.2010.01510.x

Johnston, Peter H. *Choice Words: How Our Language Affects Children's Learning*. Portland, ME: Stenhouse Publishers, 2003.

Kaup, Barbara. "What Psycholinguistic Negation Research Tells Us About the Nature of the Working-Memory Representations Utilized in Language Comprehension." In *Language and Memory: Aspects of Knowledge Representation*, 313-356. Edited by Hanna Pishwa. Berlin: De Gruyter Mouton, 2006. doi:10.1515/9783110895087.313

Kogan, Jennifer. "Brené Brown: Be the Adult You Want Your Children To Be." *Washington Post* October 5, 2012. https://www.washingtonpost.com/blogs/on-parenting/post/brene-brown-be-the-adult-you-want-your-children-to-be/2012/10/04/b5bdbd9c-0ca6-11e2-a310-2363842b7057_blog.html

Kolodner, Meredith. "NYC's Bold Gamble: Spend Big on Impoverished Students' Social and Emotional Needs to Get Academic Gains." *Hechinger Report*, Feb 9, 2017. http://hechingerreport.org/nycs-bold-gamble-spend-big-on-impoverished-students-social-and-emotional-needs-to-get-academic-gains/

Kuhl, P. K. "Is Speech Learning 'Gated' by the Social Brain?" *Developmental Science* 10, no. 1 (2007): 110–120.

Kuhl, P. K., F. M. Tsao, and H. M. Liu. "Foreign-language experience in infancy: Effects of short-term exposure and social interaction on phonetic learning." *Proceedings of the National Academy of Sciences* 100, no. 15 (2003): 9096–9101.

Kuhl, Patricia K., Rey R. Ramírez, Alexis Bosseler, Jo-Fu L. Lin. and Toshiaki Imada, "Infants' Brain Responses to Speech Suggest Analysis by Synthesis." *Proceedings of the National Academy of Sciences* 111, no. 31 (2014): 11238–11245. doi:10.1073/pnas.1410963111

Kuhl, Patricia. "The Linguistic Genius of Babies." Filmed October 2011 at TEDx Ranier. Video, 10:17. https://www.ted.com/talks/patricia_kuhl_the_linguistic_genius_of_babies

Lave, Jean. *Cognition in Practice: Mind, Mathematics and Culture in Everyday Life.* Cambridge: Cambridge University Press, 1988.

Leaper, Campbell. "Parenting Girls and Boys." In *Handbook of Parenting, Volume 1, Children and Parenting Second Edition*, 189-226. Edited by Marc H. Bornstein. Mahwah, NJ: Lawrence Erlbaum, 2002.

Lewkowicz, David and Amy Hansen-Tift. "Infants Deploy Selective Attention to the Mouth of a Talking Face When Learning Speech." *Proceedings of the National Academy of Sciences* 109, no. 5 (2012): 1431-1436. doi:10.1073/pnas.1114783109

Linguistics Society of America. "How Many Languages Are There?" http://www.linguisticsociety.org/content/how-many-languages-are-there-world

Lythcott-Haims, Julie. *How to Raise an Adult: Break Free of the Overparenting Trap and Prepare Your Kid for Success.* New York: St. Martin's Press, 2015.

Massaro, Dominic W. and Michael M. Cohen. "Perceiving Talking Faces." *Current Directions in Psychological Science* 4, no. 4 (1995): 104-109.

Matacic, Catherine. "New Sign Languages Hint at How All Languages Evolve." *Science,* April 22, 2016. doi:10.1126/science.aaf9955

Matlock, Teenie. "Metaphor, Simulation, and Fictive Motion." In *Cambridge Handbook of Cognitive Linguistics*, 477-490. Edited by Barbara Dancygier. Cambridge: Cambridge University Press, 2017.

McWilliam, Donna & Christine Howe. "Enhancing Pre-schoolers' Reasoning Skills: An Intervention to Optimise the Use of Justificatory Speech Acts During Peer Interaction." *Language & Education* 18, (2004): 504-524.

Mehan, Hugh. *Learning Lessons: Social Organization in the Classroom.* Cambridge, MA: Harvard University Press, 1979.

Menn, Lise and Nina F. Dronkers. "Why There's a High Cost to Being Slow and Sounding Weird: Who Do They Think I Am?" In *Psycholinguistics: Introduction and Applications, Second Edition*, 217. Edited by Lise Menn. San Diego, CA: Plural Publishing, 2015.

Mercer, Neil, Rupert Wegerif, and Lyn Dawes. "Children's Talk and the Development of Reasoning in the Classroom." *British Educational Research Journal 25*, no. 1 (1999): 95-111.

Michael, Ali. "What Do We Tell the Children?" *Huffington Post*, November 8, 2016. Last updated November 9, 2016. https://www.huffingtonpost.com/entry/what-should-we-tell-the-children_us_5822aa90e4b033457ie0a30b

Mischel, Walter. *The Marshmallow Test: Mastering Self-Control.* New York: Little, Brown, and Co., 2014.

Moon C., R. Cooper, and W. Fifer. "Two-day-olds Prefer their Native Language." *Infant Behavior and Development* 16, (1993): 495–500.

Mundy, Liza. "Why Is Silicon Valley So Awful to Women?" *The Atlantic Magazine,* April, 2017. https://www.theatlantic.com/magazine/archive/2017/04/why-is-silicon-valley-so-awful-to-women/517788/

National Research Council. *How People Learn: Brain, Mind, Experience, and School.* Washington, DC: National Academies Press, 2000. doi:10.17226/9853

Neitzel, Carin and Anne Dopkins Stright. "Mothers' Scaffolding of Children's Problem Solving: Establishing a Foundation of Academic Self-Regulatory Competence."*Journal of Family Psychology* 17, no. 1 (2003): 147–159. doi:10.1037/0893-3200.17.1.147

Nelson, Jane. *Positive Discipline.* New York: Ballantine, 1987/2006.

Nelson, K., & R. Fivush. "The Emergence of Autobiographical Memory: A Social Cultural Developmental Theory." *Psychological Review* 111, (2004): 486 – 511.

Nelson, Katherine. "The Psychological and Social Origins of Autobiographical Memory." *Psychological Science* 4, no. 1 (1993): 7-14. doi:10.1111/j.1467-9280.1993.tb00548.x

O'Neal, Elizabeth, Jodi Plumert, and Carole Peterson. "Parent-Child Injury Prevention Conversations Following a Trip to the Emergency Room." *Journal of Pediatric Psychology* (2015): 1-9. doi:10.1093/jpepsy/jsv070

Pons, Ferran, Laura Bosch, and David J. Lewkowicz. "Bilingualism Modulates Infants' Selective Attention to the Mouth of a Talking Face." *Psychological Science* 26, no. 4 (2015): 490-498. doi:10.1177/0956797614568320

Popova, Maria. "How We Got 'Please' and 'Thank You': Why the Line Between Politeness and Bossiness is a Linguistic Mirage." *Brain Pickings.* Accessed November 1, 2017.

https://www.brainpickings.org/2013/07/25/origin-of-please-and-thank-you/

Positive Coaching Alliance. "Attitude and Behavioral Changes in Dallas Independent School District Middle-School Athletes." Accessed November 1, 2017. https://positivecoach.org/the-power-of-positive/impact-evaluation

Ruiz, don Miguel. *The Four Agreements: A Practical Guide to Personal Freedom.* San Rafael, CA: Amber-Allen Publishing, 2003.

Schwartz, Dan and Denise Pope. "We're 'Breeding the Desire for Autonomy Out of Our Kids': Julie Lythcott-Haims on Overparenting." Produced by Stanford Radio. *School's In.* April 2, 2017. Podcast, MP3 Audio 28:35, Accessed November 1, 2017. https://ed.stanford.edu/news/we-seem-be-breeding-desire-autonomy-right-out-our-kids-julie-lythcott-haims-helicopter

Seligman, Martin. *Flourish: A Visionary New Understanding of Happiness and Well-Being.* New York: Simon and Schuster, 2011.

—. *The Optimistic Child: A Proven Program to Safeguard Children Against Depression and Build Lifelong Resilience.* New York: Houghton Mifflin, 1995, 2007.

Seppälä, Emma. "Understand the Kindness Edge: Why Compassion Serves You Better Than Self-Interest." in *The Happiness Track.* New York: Harper Collins, 2016.

—. "When Grit Goes Wrong and What to Do Instead." *Psychology Today*, May 30, 2017. https://www.psychologytoday.com/blog/feeling-it/201705/when-grit-goes-wrong-and-what-do-instead

Shipp, Josh. "Every Kid is One Caring Adult Away From Being a Success Story." Accessed November 1, 2017. Joshshipp.com.

Sinclair, J. McH. and R. M. Coulthard. *Towards an Analysis of Discourse: The English Used by Teachers and Pupils.* Oxford: Oxford University Press, 1975.

Sun, Y. and Y. Li. "Parental Divorce, Sibship Size, Family Resources, and Children's Academic Performance." *Social Science Research* 38, (2009): 622-634.

—. "Stable Postdivorce Family Structures During Late Adolescence and Socioeconomic Consequences in Adulthood." *Journal of Marriage and Family* 70, (2008): 129-143.

Tian, Ye, and Richard Breheny. "Dynamic Pragmatic View of Negation Processing" In *Negation and Polarity: Experimental Perspectives, Language, Cognition, and Mind, vol 1,* 21-43. Edited by P. Larrivée and C. Lee. Springer, Cham, 2016.

Tough, Paul. *Helping Children Succeed: What Works and Why*. New York: Houghton Mifflin Harcourt, 2016.

Vouloumanos, Athena and Janet Werker. "Listening to Language at Birth: Evidence for a Bias for Speech in Neonates." *Developmental Science* 10, no. 2 (2007): 159-164.

Wallace, Kelly. "The 'Boys are Better at Math' Mindset Creates Gender Gap in Sciences." *CNN* (October 12, 2016). http://www.cnn.com/2016/10/12/health/female-scientists-engineers-math-gender-gap/index.html

Weikum, Whitney, Athena Vouloumanos, Jordi Navarro, Salvador Soto-Faraco, Núria Sebastián-Gallés, and Janet Werker. "Visual Language Discrimination in Infancy." *Science* 316, no. 5828 (2007): 1159.

Werker, Janet and Judit Gervain. "Speech Perception in Infancy: A Foundation for Language Acquisition." *Oxford Handbook of Developmental Psychology, Volume 1: Body and Mind*. Edited by Philip D. Zelazo (2013). doi:10.1093/oxfordhb/9780199958450.013.0031

Yurovsky, Daniel, Sarah Case, and Michael C. Frank. "Preschoolers Flexibly Adapt to Linguistic Input in a Noisy Channel." *Psychological Science* 28, no 1. (2016): 132 – 140. doi:10.1177/0956797616668557

About the Author

Muffie Waterman is a mother of two teens who holds her PhD in Learning Sciences from Stanford University's Graduate School of Education. She taught courses in child and cognitive development for eight years at San Jose State University, to almost fourteen hundred undergraduate students. She has been involved in innovative education for over twenty years, working in classrooms for infant, preschool, elementary, and middle school–age students. She's taught workshops to preservice and inservice teachers. Most recently, she was Executive Director of 10 Books a Home, a nonprofit home tutoring program for high poverty families.

Muffie is passionate about bridging research and actual practice. Science has revealed a lot about how children's minds develop, but that only matters where it's actually applied—in the lives of real children, at home and in their classrooms.

Muffie resides in the San Francisco Bay Area with her husband, teenage daughter and son, one cat, and a rabbit. She loves to play, hike, do yoga, and read. People who knew her then will confirm—she had too much to say as a kid.